George Brown Goode

The beginnings of American science.

The third century. An address delivered at the eighth anniversary meeting

of the Biological society of Washington

George Brown Goode

The beginnings of American science.
The third century. An address delivered at the eighth anniversary meeting of the Biological society of Washington

ISBN/EAN: 9783337717247

Printed in Europe, USA, Canada, Australia, Japan

Cover: Foto ©ninafisch / pixelio.de

More available books at **www.hansebooks.com**

THE BEGINNINGS

OF

AMERICAN SCIENCE.

THE THIRD CENTURY.

AN ADDRESS DELIVERED AT THE EIGHTH ANNIVERSARY
MEETING OF THE BIOLOGICAL SOCIETY
OF WASHINGTON.

BY

G. BROWN GOODE,

PRESIDENT OF THE SOCIETY.

From the Proceedings of the Biological Society of Washington, Volume IV, 1886–1888.

WASHINGTON:
PRINTED FOR THE SOCIETY.
1888.

THE BEGINNINGS OF AMERICAN SCIENCE.*
THE THIRD CENTURY.

By G. Brown Goode.

VIII.

In the address which it was my privilege, one year ago, to read
in the presence of this Society, I attempted to trace the progress
of scientific activity in America from the time of the first settle-
ment by the English in 1585 to the end of the Revolution—a
period of nearly two hundred years.

Resuming the subject, I shall now take up the consideration
of the third century—from 1782 to the present time. For con-
venience of discussion the time is divided, approximately, into
decades, while the decades naturally fall into groups of three.
From 1780 to 1810, from 1810 to 1840, from 1840 to 1870, and
from 1870 to the close of the century, are periods in the history
of American thought, each of which seems to be marked by
characteristics of its own. These must have names, and it may
not be inappropriate to call the first the period of Jefferson, the
second that of Silliman, and the third that of Agassiz.

The first was, of course, an extension of the period of Linnæus,
the second and third were during the mental supremacy of Cuvier
and Von Baer and their schools, and the fourth or present, begin-
ing in 1870, belongs to that of Darwin, the extension of whose
influence to America was delayed by the tumults of the civil con-
vulsion which began in 1861 and ended in 1865.

The "beginnings of American science" do not belong entirely

---

* Annual Presidential Address delivered at the Seventh Anniversary
Meeting of the Biological Society of Washington, January 22, 1887, in
the Lecture Room of the U. S. National Museum.

to the past. Our science is still in its youth, and in the discussion of its history I shall not hesitate to refer to institutions and to tendencies which are of very recent origin.

It is somewhat unfortunate that the account book of national progress was so thoroughly balanced in the Centennial year. It is true that the movement which resulted in the birth of our Republic first took tangible form in 1776, but the infant nation was not born until 1783, when the treaty of Paris was signed, and lay in swaddling clothes until 1789, when the Constitution was adopted by the thirteen States.

In those days our forefathers had quite enough to do in adapting their lives to the changed conditions of existence. The masses were struggling for securer positions near home, or were pushing out beyond the frontiers to find dwelling-places for themselves and their descendants. The men of education were involved in political discussions as fierce, uncandid, and unphilosophical in spirit as those which preceded the French revolution of the same period.

The master minds were absorbed in political and administrative problems, and had little time for the peaceful pursuits of science, and many of the men who were prominent in science— Franklin, Jefferson, Rush, Mitchill, Seybert, Williamson, Morgan, Clinton, Rittenhouse, Patterson, Williams, Cutler, Maclure, and others—were elected to Congress or called to other positions of official responsibility.

IX.

The literary and scientific activities of the infant nation were for many years chiefly concentrated in Philadelphia, until 1800 the federal capital and largest of American cities. Here, after the return of Franklin from France in 1785, the meetings of the American Philosophical Society were resumed. Franklin continued to be its president until his death in 1790, at the same time holding the presidency of the commonwealth of Pennsylvania, and a seat in the Constitutional Convention. The prestige of its leader doubtless gave to the Society greater prominence than its scientific objects alone would have secured.

In the reminiscences of Dr. Manasseh Cutler there is to be found an admirable picture of Franklin in 1787. As we read it we are taken back into the very presence of the philosopher and statesman, and can form a very clear appreciation of the scientific atmosphere which surrounded the scientific leaders of the post-Revolutionary period.

Dr. Cutler wrote:

"Dr. Franklin lives on Market street. His house stands up a court at some distance from the street. We found him in his garden sitting upon a grass-plot, under a large mulberry tree, with several gentlemen and two or three ladies. When Mr. Gerry introduced me he rose from his chair, took me by the hand, expressed his joy at seeing me, welcomed me to the city, and begged me to seat myself close by him. His voice was low, his countenance open, frank, and pleasing. I delivered to him my letters. After he had read them he took me again by the hand and, with the usual compliments, introduced me to the other gentlemen, who are, most of them, members of the Convention. Here we entered into a free conversation, and spent the time most agreeably until it was quite dark. The tea-table was spread under the tree, and Mrs. Bache, who is the only daughter of the Doctor and lives with him, served it to the company.

"The Doctor showed me a curiosity which he had just received and with which he was much pleased. It was a snake with two heads, preserved in a large vial. It was about ten inches long, well proportioned, the heads perfect, and united to the body about one-fourth of an inch below the extremities of the jaws. He showed me a drawing of one entirely similar, found near Lake Champlain. He spoke of the situation of this snake if it was travelling among bushes, and one head should choose to go on one side of the stem of a bush and the other head should prefer the other side, and neither head would consent to come back or give way to the other. He was then going to mention a humorous matter that had that day occurred in the Convention in consequence of his comparing the snake to America; for he seemed to forget that everything in the Convention was to be kept a profound secret. But this was suggested to him, and I was deprived of the story.

" After it was dark we went into the house, and he invited me to
his library, which is likewise his study.   It is a very large chamber and high-studded.   The walls are covered with shelves filled
with books ; beside these, four large alcoves, extending two-thirds
the length of the chamber, filled in the same manner. I presume
this is the largest and by far the best private library in America.
He showed me a glass machine for exhibiting the circulation of
the blood in the arteries and veins of the human body. The circulation is exhibited by the passing of a red fluid from a reservoir
into numerous capillary tubes of glass, ramified in every direction,
and then returning in similar tubes to the reservoir, which was
done with great velocity, and without any power acting visibly
upon the fluid, and had the appearance of perpetual motion.
Another great curiosity was a rolling press for taking copies of
letters or other writing.   A sheet of paper is completely copied
in two minutes, the copy as fair as the original, and without de-
facing it in the smallest degree.   It is an invention of his own,
extremely useful in many circumstances of life.   He also showed
us his long artificial hand and arm for taking down and putting
up books on high shelves, out of reach, and his great arm-chair,
with rockers and a large fan placed over it, with which he fans
himself, while he sits reading, with only a slight motion of the
foot, and many other curiosities and inventions, all his own, but
of lesser note.   Over his mantel he has a prodigious number of
medals, busts, and casts in wax or plaster of Paris, which are the
effigies of the most noted characters of Europe.   But what the
Doctor wished especially to show me was a huge volume on botany, which indeed afforded me the greatest pleasure of any one
thing in his library.   It was a single volume, but so large that it
was with great difficulty that he was able to raise it from a low
shelf and lift it to the table ; but, with that senile ambition which
is common to old people (Dr. Franklin was eighty-one), he insisted on doing it himself, and would permit no one to assist him,
merely to show how much strength he had remaining.   It contained the whole of Linnæus's Systema Vegetabilium, with large
cuts colored from nature of every plant.   It was a feast to me,
and the Doctor seemed to enjoy it as well as myself.   We spent
a couple of hours examining this volume, while the other gentlemen amused themselves with other matters.   The Doctor is not
a botanist, but lamented he did not in early life attend to this
science.   He delights in natural history, and expressed an earnest
wish that I should pursue a plan I had begun, and hoped this
science, so much neglected in America, would be pursued with
as much ardor here as it is now in every part of Europe.   I
wanted, for three months at least, to have devoted myself entirely
to this one volume, but, fearing lest I should become tedious to
him, I shut the book, though he urged me to examine it longer.

He seemed extremely fond, through the course of the visit, of dwelling on philosophical subjects, and particularly that of natural history, while the other gentlemen were swallowed up in politics. This was a favorable circumstance to me, for almost all his conversation was addressed to me, and I was highly delighted with the extensive knowledge he appeared to possess of every subject, the brightness of his faculties, the clearness and vivacity of his mental powers, and the strength of his memory, notwithstanding his age. His manners are perfectly easy, and everything about him seems to diffuse an unrestrained freedom and happiness. He has an incessant vein of humor, accompanied with an uncommon vivacity that seems as natural and involuntary as his breathing."

To Franklin, as President of the Philosophical Society, succeeded David Rittenhouse [b. 1732, d. 1796], a man of world-wide reputation, known in his day as " *the* American Philosopher."*

He was an astronomer of repute, and his observatory built at Norriton in preparation for the transit of Venus in 1769 seems to have been the first in America. His orrery, constructed upon an original plan, was one of the wonders of the land. His most important contribution to astronomy was the introduction of the use of spider lines in the focus of transit instruments.†

He was an amateur botanist, and in 1771 made interesting physiological experiments upon the electric eel.‡

He was a Fellow of the Royal Society of London, and the first Director of the United States Mint.

Next in prominence to Franklin and Rittenhouse were doubtless the medical professors, Benjamin Rush, William Shippen, John Morgan, Adam Kuhn, Samuel Powell Griffiths, and Caspar Wistar, all men of scientific tastes, but too busy in public affairs and in medical instruction to engage deeply in research, for Philadelphia, in those days as at present, insisted that all

---

* See obituary in the *European Magazine*, July, 1796; also Memoirs of Rittenhouse, by WILLIAM BARTON, 1813, and Eulogium by Benjamin Rush, 1796.

† VON ZACH: Monatliche Correspondenz, ii, p. 215.

‡ Phila. Medical Repository, vol. i.

her naturalists should be medical professors, and the active investigators, outside of medical science, were not numerous. Rush, however, was one of the earliest American writers upon ethnology, and a pathologist of the highest rank. He is generally referred to as the earliest professor of chemistry, having been appointed to the chair of chemistry in the College of Philadelphia in 1769; it seems certain, however, that Dr. John Morgan lectured on chemistry as early as 1765.*

Dr. Shippen [b. 1735, d. 1808], the founder of the first medical school [1765] and its professor of anatomy for forty-three years, was still in his prime, and so was Dr. Morgan [b. 1735, d. 1789], a Fellow of the Royal Society, a co-founder of the medical school, and a frequent contributor to the Philosophical Transactions. Morgan was an eminent pathologist, and is said to have been the one to originate the theory of the formation of pus by the secretory action of the vessels of the part.† He appears to have been the first who attempted to form a museum of anatomy, having learned the methods of preparation from the Hunters and from Süe in Paris. The beginning was still earlier known, for a collection of anatomical models in wax, obtained by Dr. Abraham Chovet in Paris, was in use by Philadelphia medical students before the Revolution.‡

Another of the physicians of colonial days who lived until after the revolution was Dr. Thomas Cadwallader [b. 1707, d. 1779], whose dissections are said to have been among the earliest made in America, and whose " Essay on the West India Dry Gripes," 1775, was one of the earliest medical treatises in America.

Dr. Caspar Wistar [b. 1761, d. 1818] was also a leader,

---

* Barton's Memoirs of Rittenhouse, p. 614.

† Thacher. American Medical Biography, i. p. 408.

‡ This eventually became the property of the University. See Barton's Rittenhouse, p. 377. Trans. Amer. Phil. Soc., ii, p. 368.

and was at various times professor of chemistry and anatomy. His contributions to natural history were descriptions of bones of *Megalonyx* and other mammals, a study of the human ethmoid, and experiments on evaporation. He was long Vice-President of the Philosophical Society, and in 1815 succeeded Jefferson in its presidency. The Wistar Anatomical Museum of the University · and the beautiful climbing shrub *Wistaria* are among the memorials to his name.*

Still another memorial of the venerable naturalist may perhaps be worthy of mention as an illustration of the social conditions of science in Philadelphia in early days. A traveller visiting the city in 1829 thus described this institution, which was continued until the late war, and then discontinued, but has been resumed within the last year :

" Dr. Wistar in his lifetime had a party of his literary and scientific friends at his house, one evening in each week, and to this party strangers visiting the city were also invited. When he died, the same party was continued. and the members of the Wistar party, in their turn, each have a meeting of the club at his house, on some Saturday night in the year. This club consists of the men most distinguished in science, art, literature, and wealth in the city. It opens at early candle-light, when not only the members themselves appear, but they bring with them all the strangers of distinction in the city."†

The " Wistar parties " were continued up to the beginning of the civil war in 1861, and have been resumed since 1887. A history of these gatherings would cover a period of three-quarters of a century at the least, and could be made a most valuable and entertaining contribution to scientific literature.

Packard, in his History of Zoölogy,‡ states that zoölogy, the world over, has sprung from the study of human anatomy, and

---

* HOSACK : Tribute to the Memory of Wistar, New York, 1818.
† ATWATER : Remarks made on a tour to Prairie du Chién ; thence to Washington City, in 1829. Columbus, 1831, p. 238.
‡ Standard Natural History, pp. lxii–lxxii.

that American zoölogy took its rise, and was fostered chiefly, in Philadelphia, by the professors in the medical schools. It was fully demonstrated, I think, in my former address, that there were good zoölogists in America long before there were medical schools, and that Philadelphia was *not* the cradle of American natural history; although, during its period of political pre-eminence, immediately after the Revolution, scientific activities of all kinds centred in that city. As for the medical schools it is at least probable that they have spoiled more naturalists than they have fostered.

Dr. Adam Kuhn [b. 1741, d. 1817] was the professor of botany in 1768 *—the first in America—and was labeled by his contemporaries " the favorite pupil of Linnæus." Professor Gray, in a recent letter to the writer, refers to this saying as a " myth;" and it surely seems strange that a disciple beloved by the great Swede could have done so little for botany. Barton, in a letter, in 1792, to Thunberg, who then occupied the seat of Linnæus in the University of Upsala, said:

" The electricity of your immortal Linné has hardly been felt in this Ultima Thule of science. Had a number of the pupils of that great man settled in North America its riches would have been better known. But, alas! the only one pupil of your predecessor that has made choice of America as the place of his residence has added nothing to the stock of natural knowledge."†

The Rev. Nicholas Collin, Rector of the Swedish Churches in Pennsylvania, was a fellow-countryman and acquaintance of Linnæus‡ and an accomplished botanist, having been one of the editors of Muhlenberg's work upon the grasses and an early writer on American linguistics. He read before the Philosophical Society, in 1789, "An Essay on those inquiries in

* See p. 99, *ante.*

† B. S. BARTON, in Transactions American Philosophical Society, iii, p. 339.

‡ "I often heard the great Linnæus wish that he could have explored the continent of North America." COLLIN: Trans. Amer. Phil. Soc., iii, p. xv.

Natural Philosophy which at present are most beneficial to the United States of North America," which was the first attempt to lay out a systematic plan for the direction of scientific research in America. One of the most interesting suggestions he made was that the Mammoth was still in existence.

" The vast Mahmot," said he, " is perhaps yet stalking through the western wilderness; but if he is no more let us carefully gather his remains, and even try to find a new skeleton of this giant, to whom the elephant was but a calf." *

Gen. Jonathan Williams, U. S. A. [b. 1750, d. 1815], was first superintendent of the Military Academy at West Point and " father of the corps of engineers." He was a nephew of Franklin, and his secretary of legation in France, and, after his return to Philadelphia, was for many years a judge of the court of common pleas, his military career not beginning till 1801. This versatile man was a leading member of the Philosophical Society and one of its Vice-Presidents. His paper " On the Use of the Thermometer in Navigation " was one of the first American contributions to scientific seamanship.

The Rev. Dr. John Ewing [b. 1732, d. 1802], also a Vice-President, was Provost of the University. He had been one of the observers of the transit in 1769, of which he published an account in the Transactions of the Philosophical Society. He early printed a volume of lectures on Natural Philosophy, and was the strongest champion of John Godfrey, the Philadelphian, in his claim to the invention of the reflecting quadrant.†

---

* *Id.*, p. xxiv.

† "Thomas Godfrey," says a recent authority, "was born in Bristol, Penn., in 1704, and died in Philadelphia in December, 1749. He followed the trade of a glazier in the metropolis, and, having a fondness for mathematical studies, marked such books as he met with, subsequently acquiring Latin, that he might become familiar with the mathematical work in that language. Having obtained a copy of Newton's ' Principia,' he described an improvement he had made in Davis' quadrant to James Logan,

Dr. James Woodhouse [b. 1770, d. 1809] was author and editor of several chemical text-books and Professor of Chemistry in the University, a position which he took after it had been refused by Priestley. He made experiments and observations on the vegetation of plants, and investigated the chemical and medical properties of the persimmon tree. He it was who first demonstrated the superiority of anthracite to bituminous coal by reason of its intensity and regularity of heating power.*

The Rev. Ebenezer Kinnersley [b. in Gloucester, England, Nov. 30, 1711, d. in Philadelphia, July 4, 1778] survived the Revolution, though, in his latter years, not a contributor to science. The associate of Franklin in " the Philadelphia Experiments " in electricity, his discoveries were famous in Europe as well as in America.† It is claimed that he originated the theory of the positive and negative in electricity; that he first demonstrated the passage of electricity through water; and that he first discovered that heat could be produced by electricity; besides inventing numerous mechanical devices of scientific interest. From 1753 to 1772 he was connected with the University of Pennsylvania, where there may still be seen a window dedicated to his memory.

Having already referred to the history of scientific instruction in America,‡ and shown that Hunter lectured on comparative anatomy in Newport in 1754; Kuhn on Botany, in Philadelphia, in 1768, Waterhouse on natural history and botany, at Cambridge, in 1788; and some unidentified scholars upon chemistry and natural history, in Philadelphia, in 1785, it would seem unjust not to speak of Kinnersley's career as a lecturer.

---

who was so impressed that he at once addressed a letter to Edmund Halley in England, giving a full description of the construction and uses of Godfrey's instrument."

* SILLIMAN : American Contributions to Chemistry, p. 13.

† See *Priestley's* History of Electricity.

‡ P. 99, *ante.*

He seems to have been the first to deliver public scientific lectures in America, occupying the platform in Philadelphia, Newport, New York, and Boston, from 1751 to the beginning of the Revolution. The following advertisement was printed in the "Pennsylvania Gazette" for April 11, 1751 :

> NOTICE is hereby given to the *Curious* that Wednesday next Mr. Kinnersley proposes to begin a Course of Experiments on the newly-discovered *Electrical Fire*, containing not only the most curious of those that have been made and published in Europe, but a considerable Number of New Ones lately made in this City, to be accompanied with methodical *Lectures* on the Nature and Properties of that Wonderful Element.

Francis Hopkinson [b. 1737, d. 1791], signer of the Declaration of Independence, was treasurer of the Philosophical Society, and among other papers communicated by him was one in 1783, calling attention to the peculiar worm parasitic in the eye of a horse. The "horse with a snake in its eye" was on public exhibition in Philadelphia in 1782, and was the object of much attention, for the nature and habits of this peculiar *Filaria* were not so well understood then as now.

The father of Francis, Thomas Hopkinson [b. in London, 1709, d. in Philadelphia, 1751], who was overlooked in my previous address, deserves, at least, a passing mention. Coming to Philadelphia in 1731 he became lawyer, prothonotary, Judge of the Admiralty, and member of the Provincial Council. As an incorporator of the Philadelphia Library Company, and original trustee of the College of Philadelphia, and first President of the American Philosophical Society in 1743, his public spirit is worthy of our admiration. He was associated with Kinnersley and Franklin in the "Philadelphia Experiments;" and Franklin said of him :

" The power of points to throw off the electrical fire was first communicated to me by my ingenious friend, Mr. Thomas Hopkinson." *

---

* WILSON & FISKE : Cyclopædia of American Biography, iii, 260.

The name of Philip Syng is also mentioned in connection with the Philadelphia experiments, and it would be well if some memorials of his work could be placed upon record.

William Bartram [b. 1739, d. 1823] was living in the famous botanical garden at Kingsessing, which his father, the old King's botanist, had bequeathed him in 1777. He was for some years professor of botany in the Philadelphia college, and in 1791 printed his charming volume descriptive of his travels in Florida, the Carolinas, and Georgia. The latter years of his life appear to have been devoted to quiet observation. William · Bartram has been, perhaps, as much underrated as John Bartram has been unduly exalted. He was one of the best observers America has ever produced, and his book, which rapidly passed through several editions in English and French, is a classic and should stand beside White's "Selborne" in every naturalist's library. Bartram was doubtless discouraged early in his career by the failure of his patrons in London to make any scientific use of the immense botanical collections made by him in the South before the Revolution, which, many years later, was lying unutilized in the Banksian herbarium. Coues has called attention very emphatically to the merits of his bird work, which he pronounces "the starting-point of a distinctly American school of ornithology." Two of the most eminent of our early zoölogists, Wilson and Say, were his pupils; the latter his kinsman, and the former his neighbor, were constantly with him at Kingsessing and drew much of their inspiration from his conversation. "Many birds which Wilson first fully described and figured were really named and figured by Bartram in his Travels, and several of his designations were simply adopted by Wilson."*

Bartram's "Observations on the Creek and Cherokee Indians"†

---

* COUES: Key to North American Birds, p. xvi
† Trans. Am. Ethnological Society, iii, 1851.

was an admirable contribution to ethnography, and his general observations were of the highest value.

In the introduction to his " Travels," and interspersed through this volume, are reflections which show him to have been the possessor of a very philosophic and original mind. His "Anecdotes of an American Crow " and his " Memoirs of John Bartram "* were worthy products of his pen, while his illustrations to Barton's " Elements of Botany " show how facile and truthful was his pencil.

His love for botany was such, we are told, that he wrote a description of a plant only a few minutes before his death, a statement which will be readily believed by all who know the nature of his enthusiasm. Thus, for instance, he wrote of the Venus's Fly Trap:

"Admirable are the properties of the extraordinary Dionæa mus-cipula! See the incarnate lobes expanding; how gay and sportive they appear! ready on the spring to entrap incautious, deluded in-sects! What artifice! There! behold one of the leaves just closed upon a struggling fly; another has gotten a worm; its hold is sure; its prey can never escape—carnivorous vegetable! Can we, after viewing this object, hesitate for a moment to confess that vegeta-ble beings are endowed with some sensible faculties or attributes similar to those that dignify animal nature? They are living, or-ganical, and self-moving bodies; for we see here in this plant motion and volition."†

Moses Bartram, a cousin of William, and also a botanist. was also living near Philadelphia, and in 1879 published "Observa-tions on the Native Silk Worms of North America," and Hum-phrey Marshall [1722-1801], the farmer-botanist, had a botanical garden of his own, and in 1785 published " The American Grove—Arbustrium Americanum "—a treatise on the forest trees and shrubs of the United States, which was the first strictly

---

* Nicholson's Journal, 1805.
† Travels, 1793, p. xiv.

American botanical book, and which was republished in France a few years later in 1789.

Gotthilf Muhlenberg [b. 1753, d. 1815], a Lutheran clergyman, living at Lancaster, was an eminent botanist, educated in Germany, though a native of Pennsylvania. His " Flora of Lancaster " was a pioneer work In 1813 he published a full catalogue of the Plants of North America, in which about 2,800 species were mentioned. He supplied Hedwig with many of the rare American mosses, which were published either in " Stirpes Cryptogamicæ " of that author or in the " Species Muscorum." To Sir J. E. Smith and Mr. Dawson Turner he likewise sent many plants. He made extensive preparations, writing a general flora of North America, but death interfered with his[1] project. The American Philosophical Society preserves his herbarium, and the moss *Funeria Muhlenbergii*, the violet, *Viola Muhlenbergii*, and the grass *Muhlenbergia*, are among the memorials to his name.*

To Pennsylvania, but not to Philadelphia, came, in 1794, Joseph Priestley (1733–1804), the philosopher, theologian, and chemist. Although his name is more famous in the history of chemistry than that of any living contemporary, American or European, his work was nearly finished before he left England. He never entered into the scientific life of the country which he sought as an exile, and of which he never became a citizen, and he is not properly to be considered an element in the history of American science.

His coming, however, was an event of considerable political importance ; and William Cobbett's " Observations on the Emigration of Doctor Joseph Priestley. By Peter Porcupine," was followed by several other pamphlets equally vigorous in expression. McMaster is evidently unjust to some of the public

---

* HOOKER : On the Botany of America. Edinburgh Journal of Science, iii, p. 103, *et seq.*

men who welcomed Priestley to America, though no one will
deny that there were unprincipled demagogues in America in
the year of grace 1794.   Jefferson was undoubtedly sincere when
he wrote to him the words quoted elsewhere in this address.

Another eminent exile, welcomed by Jefferson, and the writer,
at the President's request, of a work on national education in the
United States, was M. Pierre Samuel Dupont de Nemours [b. in
Paris, 1799, d. 1817].   He was a member of the Institute of
France, a statesman, diplomatist, and political economist, and
author of many important works.   He lived in the United States
at various times, from 1799 to 1817, when he died near
Wilmington, Delaware.   Like Priestley, he was a member of the
American Philosophical Society, and affiliated with its leading
members.

The gunpowder works near Wilmington, Delaware, founded
by his son in 1798, are still of great importance, and the statue
of one of his grandsons, an Admiral in the U. S. Navy, adorns
one of the principal squares in the National Capital.

Among other notable names on the roll of the society, in the
last century, were those of Gen. Anthony Wayne and Thomas
Payne. His Excellency General Washington was also an active
member, and seems to have taken sufficient interest in the society
to nominate for foreign membership the Earl of Buchan, President of the Society of Scottish Antiquarians, and Dr. James Anderson, of Scotland.

The following note written by Washington is published in the
Memoirs of Rittenhouse :

" The President presents his compliments to Mr. Rittenhouse,
and thanks him for the attention he has given to the case of Mr.
Anderson and the Earl of Buchan.
" SUNDAY AFTERNOON, 20*th April*, 1794."

Of all the Philadelphia naturalists of those early days, the one
who had the most salutary influence upon the progress of science

was, perhaps, Benjamin Smith Barton [b. 1766, d. 1815.] Barton was the nephew of Rittenhouse, and the son of the Rev. Thomas Barton, a learned Episcopal Clergyman of Lancaster, who was one of the earliest members of the Philosophical Society, and a man accomplished in science.

He studied at Edinburgh and Göttingen, and at the age of 19, in 1785, he was the assistant of Rittenhouse and Ellicott, in the work of establishing the western boundary of Pennsylvania, and soon after was sent to Europe, whence, having pursued an extended course of scientific and medical study, he returned in 1789, and was elected professor of natural history and botany in the University of Pennsylvania. He was a leader in the Philosophical Society, and the founder of the Linnæan Society of Philadelphia, before which, in 1807, he delivered his famous " Discourse on some of the Principal Desiderata in Natural History," which did much to excite an intelligent popular interest in the subject. His essays upon natural history topics were the first of the kind to appear in this country. He belonged to the school of Gilbert White and Benjamin Stillingfleet, and was the first in America of a most useful and interesting group of writers, among whom may be mentioned John D. Godman, Samuel Lockwood, C. C. Abbott, Nicholas Pike, John Burroughs, Wilson Flagg, Ernest Ingersoll, the Rev. Dr. McCook, Hamilton Gibson, Maurice Thompson, and W. T. Hornaday, as well as Matthew Jones, Campbell Hardy, Charles Waterton, P. H. Gosse, and Grant Allen, to whom America and England both have claims.

Barton published certain descriptive papers, as well as manuals of botany and materia medica, but in latter life had become so absorbed in medical affairs that he appears to have taken no interest in the struggles of the infant Academy of Natural Sciences, which was founded three years before his death, but of which he never became a member.

His nephew and successor in the Presidency of the Linnæan Society and the University Professorship, William P. C. Barton [b. 1786, d. 1856], was a man of similar tendencies, who in early life published papers on the flora of Philadelphia [Floræ Philadelphiæ Prodromus, 1815], but later devoted himself chiefly to professional affairs, writing copiously upon materia medica and medical botany.

The admirers of Benjamin Smith Barton have called him "the father of American Natural History," but I cannot see the propriety of this designation, which is equally applicable to Mitchill or Jefferson, and perhaps still more so to Peter Collinson, of London. The praises of Barton have been so well and so often sung that I do not feel guilty of injustice in passing him briefly by.*

The most remarkable naturalist of those days was Rafinesque, [b. 1784, d. 1872], a Sicilian by birth, who came to Philadelphia in 1802.

Nearly fifty years ago this man died, friendless and impoverished, in Philadelphia. His last words were these : " Time renders justice to all at last." Perhaps the day has not yet come when full justice can be done to the memory of Constantine Rafinesque, but his name seems yearly to grow more prominent in the history of American zoölogy. He was in many respects the most gifted man who ever stood in our ranks. When in his prime he far surpassed his American contemporaries in versatility and comprehensiveness of grasp. He lived a century too soon. His spirit was that of the present period. In the latter years of his life, soured by disappointments, he seemed to become unsettled in mind, but as I read the story of his life his eccentricities seem to me the outcome of a boundless enthusiasm for the study of nature. The picturesque events of his life have

* W. P. C. BARTON: Biography of Benjamin S. Barton, Philadelphia, 1815

been so well described by Jordan,* Chase,† and Audubon‡ that they need not be referred to here. The most satisfactory gauge of his abilities is perhaps his masterly " Survey of the Progress and Actual State of Natural Sciences in the United States of America," printed in 1817.§ His own sorrowful estimate of the outcome of his mournful career is very touching :

"I have often been discouraged, but have never despaired long. I have lived to serve mankind, but have often met with ungrateful returns. I have tried to enlarge the limits of knowledge, but have often met with jealous rivals instead of friends. With a greater fortune I might have imitated Humboldt or Linnæus."

Dr. Robert Hare [b. 1781, d. 1858] began his long career of usefulness in 1801, at the age of twenty, by the invention of the oxyhydrogen blow-pipe. This was exhibited at a meeting of the Chemical Society of Philadelphia in 1801.‖

This apparatus was perhaps the most remarkable of his original contributions to science, which he continued without interruption for more than fifty years. It belongs to the end of the post-revolutionary period, and is therefore noticed, although it is not the purpose of this essay to consider in detail the work of the specialists of the present century.

Dr. Hugh Williamson [b. Dec. 5, 1735, d., in New York, May 22, 1719] was a prominent but not particularly useful promoter of science, a writer rather than a thinker. His work has already been referred to. The names of Maclure, who came to Philadelphia about 1797, the Rev. John Heckewelder, and Albert Gallatin [b. 1761, d. in 1849], a native of Switzerland, a statesman and financier, subsequently identified with the scientific cir-

---

* JORDAN : Bulletin xv, U. S. National Museum : Science Sketches, p. 143.
† CHASE : Potter's American Monthly, vi, pp. 97–101.
‡ AUDUBON : The Eccentric Naturalist < Ornithological Biography, p. 455.
§ Amer. Monthly Magazine, ii, 81.
‖ Amer. Month. Mag., i, 80.

cles of New York, complete the list of the Philadelphia savans of the last century.

There is not in all American literature a passage which illustrates the peculiar tendencies in the thought of this period so thoroughly as Jefferson's defense of the country against the charges of Buffon and Raynal, which he published in 1783, which is particularly entertaining because of its almost pettish depreciation of our motherland.

"On doit etre etonné" (says Raynal) " que l'Amerique n'ait pas encore produit un bon poëte, un habile mathematicien, un homme de génie dans un seul art ou un seule science."

"When we shall have existed a people as long as the Greeks did before they produced a Homer, the Romans a Virgil, the French a Racine and Voltaire, the English a Shakespeare and Milton, should this reproach still be true, we will inquire from what unfriendly causes it has proceeded that the other countries of Europe and quarters of the earth shall not have inscribed any name on the rôle of poets.

" In war we have produced a *Washington* whose name will in future ages assume its just station among the celebrated worthies of the world, when that wretched philosophy shall be forgotten which would have arranged him among the degeneracies of nature.

" In physics we have produced a *Franklin*, than whom no one of the present age has made more important discoveries, nor has enriched philosophy with more, or more ingenious, solutions of the phænomena of nature.

" We have supposed *Mr. Rittenhouse* second to no astronomer living ; that in genius he must be the first because he is self-taught. He has not indeed made a world ; but he has by imitation approached nearer its Maker than any man who has lived from the creation to this day. There are various ways of keeping the truth out of sight. Mr. Rittenhouse's model of the planetary system has the plagiary appellation of an orrery ; and the quadrant invented by *Godfrey*, an American also, and with the aid of which the European nations traverse the globe, is called Hadley's quadrant.

" We calculate thus : The United States contain three millions of inhabitants ; France twenty millions ; and the British Islands ten. We produce a Washington, a Franklin, a Rittenhouse. France then should have half a dozen in each of these lines, and Great Britain half that number, equally eminent. It may be true that France has; we are but just becoming acquainted with her, and our acquaintance so far gives us high ideas of the genius of her inhabitants.

" The present war having so long cut off all communications with Great Britain, we are not able to make a fair estimate of the state of science in that country. The spirit in which she wages war is the only sample before our eyes, and that does not seem the legitimate offspring either of science or civilization. The sun of her glory is fast descending to the horizon. Her philosophy has crossed the channel, her freedom the Atlantic, and herself seems bearing to that awful dissolution whose issue is not given human forethought to scan."*

This was one phase of public sentiment. Another, no less instructive, is that shown forth in the publications of Jefferson's fierce political opponents in 1790, paraphrased, as follows, by McMaster in his " History of the People of the United States : "

" Why, it was asked, should a philosopher be made President? Is not the active, anxious, and responsible station of Executive illy suited to the calm, retired, and exploring tastes of a natural philosopher? Ability to impale butterflies and contrive turn-about chairs may entitle one to a college professorship, but it no more constitutes a claim to the Presidency than the genius of Cox, the great bridge-builder, or the feats of Ricketts, the equestrian. Do not the pages of history teem with evidence of the ignorance and mismanagement of philosophical politicians? John Locke was a philosopher, and framed a constitution for the colony of Georgia, but so full was it of whimsies that it had to be thrown aside. Condorcet, in 1793, made a constitution for France, but it contained more absurdities than were ever before piled up in a system of government, and was not even tried. Rittenhouse was another philosopher; but the only proof he gave of political talents was suffering himself to be wheedled into the presidency of the Democratic Society of Philadelphia. But suppose that the title of philosopher is a good claim to the Presidency, what claim has Thomas Jefferson to the title of philosopher? Why, forsooth !

" He has refuted Moses, dishonored the story of the Deluge, made a penal code, drawn up a report in weights and measures, and speculated profoundly on the primary causes of the difference between the whites and blacks. Think of such a man as President! Think of a foreign minister surprising him in the act of anatomizing the kidneys and glands of an African to find out why the negro is black and odoriferous !

---

* Notes on Virginia, 1788, pp. 69–71.

" He has denied that shells found on the mountain tops are parts of the great flood. He has declared that if the contents of the whole atmosphere were water, the land would only be overflowed to the depth of fifty-two and a half feet. He does not believe the Indians emigrated from Asia.

" Every mail from the South brought accounts of rumblings and quakes in the Alleghanies, and strange lights and blazing meteors in the sky. These disturbances in the natural world might have no connection with the troubles in the political world; nevertheless it was impossible not to compare them with the prodigies all writers of the day declare preceded the fatal Ides of March."

X.

In New York, although a flourishing medical school had been in existence from 1769, there was an astonishing dearth of naturalists until about 1790. Governor Colden, the botanist and ethnologist, had died in 1776, and the principal medical men of the city, the Bards, Clossy, Jones, Middleton, Dyckman, and others, confined their attention entirely to professional studies. A Philosophical Society was born in 1787, but died before it could speak. A Society for the Promotion of Agriculture, Arts, and Manufactures, organized in 1791, was more successful, but not in the least scientific. Up to the end of the century New York State had but six men chosen to membership in the American Philosophical Society, and, up to 1809, but five in the American Academy. Leaders, however, soon arose in Mitchill, Clinton, and Hosack.

Samuel Latham Mitchill, the son of a Quaker farmer [b. 1764, d. 1831], was educated in the medical schools of New York and Edinburgh, and in 1792 was appointed Professor of Chemistry, Natural History, and Philosophy in Columbia College. Although during most of his long life a medical professor and editor, and for many years representative and senator in Congress, he continued active in the interests of general science. He made many contributions to systematic natural history, notably a History of the Fishes of New York, and his edition of Bewick's

" General History of Quadrupeds," published in New York in 1804, with notes and additions, and some figures of American animals, was the earliest American work of the kind. He was the first in America to lecture upon geology, and published several papers upon this science.   His " Mineralogical Exploration of the banks of the Hudson River" in 1796, under the " Society for the Promotion of Agriculture, Manufactures, and Useful Arts," founded by himself, was our earliest attempt at this kind of research, and in 1794 he published an essay on the " Nomenclature of the New Chemistry," the first American paper on chemical philosophy, and engaged in a controversy with Priestley, in defence of the nomenclature of Lavoisier, which he was the first American to adopt.

His discourse on " The Botanical History of North and South America" was also a pioneer effort. He was an early leader in ethnological inquiries and a vigorous writer on political topics. His " Life of Tammany, the Indian Chief" (New York, 1795), is a classic, and he was well known to our grandfathers as the author of " An Address to the Fredes or People of the United States," in which he proposed that " Fredonia" should be adopted as the name of the nation.

Dr. Mitchill was a poet,* and a humorist, and a member of the literary circles of his day.   In " The Croakers" Rodman Drake thus addressed him as " The Surgeon General of New York :"

> " It matters not how high or low it is
> Thou knowest each hill and vale of knowledge,
> Fellow of forty-nine societies
> And lecturer in Hosack's College."

Fitz-Greene Halleck also paid his compliments in the following terms :

> " Time was when Dr. Mitchill's word was law,
> When Monkeys, Monsters, Whales and Esquimaux,
> Asked but a letter from his ready hand,
> To be the theme and wonder of the land."

---

* Examples of his verses may be found in Duyckinck's Cyclopædia of American Literature.

These and other pleasantries, of which many are quoted in Fairchild's admirable " History of the New York Academy of Sciences," gives us an idea of the provinciality of New York sixty years ago, when every citizen would seem to have known the principal local representatives of science, and to have felt a sense of personal proprietorship in him and in his projects.

Mitchill was a leader in the New York Historical Society; founder of the Literary and Philosophical Society, and of its successor, the Lyceum of Natural History, of which he was long president. He was also President of the New York Branch of the Linnæan Society of Paris, and of the N. Y. State Medical Society, and Surgeon-General of the State Militia ; a man of the widest influence and universally beloved. He served four terms in the House of Representatives, and was five years a member of the U. S. Senate.*

DeWitt Clinton [b. 1769, d. 1828], statesman and philanthropist, U. S. Senator, and Governor of New York, was a man of similar tastes and capacities. What Benjamin Franklin was to Philadelphia in the middle of the eighteenth century DeWitt Clinton was to New York in the beginning of the nineteenth. He was the author of the Hibernicus " Letters on the Natural History and Internal Resources of the State of New York " (New York, 1822), a work of originality and merit. As President of the Literary and Philosophical Society he delivered in 1814 an " Introductory Discourse," which, like Barton's in

---

* See FRANCIS, JOHN W. Life of Dr. Mitchill, in Williams's American Medical Biography, pp. 401-411, and eulogy in Discourse in Commemoration of 53d Anniversary of N. Y. Hist. Soc., 1857, 56-60; and in his Old New York; also—

Sketch by H. L. Fairchild in History of the New York Academy of Sciences, 1887, pp. 57-67; also Dr. Mitchill's own pamphlet: Some of the Memorable Events and Occurrences in the Life of Samuel S. Mitchill, of New York, from the year 1786 to 1827.

A biography by Akerly was in existence, but has never been printed.

Numerous portraits are in existence, which are described by Fairchild.

Philadelphia, ten years before, was productive of great good. It was, moreover, laden with the results of original and important observations in all departments of natural history. Another important paper was his "Memoirs on the Antiquities of Western New York" printed in 1818.

Clinton's attention was devoted chiefly to public affairs, and especially to the organization of the admirable school system of New York and other internal improvements. He did enough in science. however, to place him in the highest ranks of our early naturalists.*

Hosack has been referred to elsewhere as a pioneer in mineralogy and the founder of the first botanic garden. He was long president of the Historical Society, and exercised a commanding influence in every direction. His researches were, however, chiefly medical.

Samuel Akerly [b. 1785, d. 1845], the brother-in-law of Mitchill, a graduate of Columbia College, 1807, was an industrious worker in zoölogy and botany and the author of the "Geology of the Hudson River." John Griscom [b. 1774, d. 1852], one of the earliest teachers of chemistry, began in 1806 a career of great usefulness. "For thirty years," wrote Francis, "he was the acknowledged head of all other teachers of chemistry among us (in New York), and he kept pace with the flood of light which Davy, Murray, Gaylussac, and Thenard, and others shed on the progress of chemical philosophy at that day." About 1820 he went abroad to study scientific institutions, and his charming book, 'A Year in Europe,' supplemented by his regular contributions to *Silliman's Journal*, commenting on scientific affairs in other countries, did much to stimulate the growth of scientific and educational institutions in America.

---

* HOSACK: Memoirs of DeWitt Clinton. New York, 1829. RENWICK: Life of DeWitt Clinton. New York, 1840. CAMPBELL: Life and Writings of DeWitt Clinton. New York, 1849.

Francis tells us that he was for thirty years the acknowledged head of the teachers of chemistry in New York.*

A zealous promoter of zoölogy in those days was F. Adrian Vanderkemp, of Oldenbarnavelt, New York, who in 1795, we are told, delivered an address before an Agricultural Society in Whitesburg, N. Y., in which he offered premiums for essays upon certain subjects, among which was one " for the best anatomical and historical account of the moose, fifty dollars, or for bringing one in alive, sixty dollars."†

Having mentioned several American naturalists of foreign birth, it may not be out of place to refer to the American origin of an English zoölogist of high repute, Dr. Thomas Horsfield, born in Philadelphia in 1773, and after many years in the East became, in 1820, a resident of London, where he died in 1859. His name is prominent among those of the entomologists, botanists, and ornithologists of this century, especially in connection with Java.

XI.

In New England, science was more highly appreciated than in New York. Massachusetts had in John Adams a man who, like Franklin and Jefferson, realized that scientific institutions were the best protection for a democratic government, and to his efforts America owes its second scientific society—the American Academy of Arts and Sciences, founded in 1780. When Mr. Adams travelled from Boston to Philadelphia, in the days just before the Revolution, he several times visited at Norwalk, we are told, a curious collection of American birds and insects made by Mr. Arnold. "This was afterwards sold to Sir Ashton Lever, in whose apartments in London Mr. Adams saw it again, and felt ı new regret at our imperfect knowledge of the productions of

---

* GRISCOM. JOHN H.: Memoir of John Griscom. New York, 1859.
† DeWitt Clinton, in Trans. Lt. Phil. Soc. N. Y., p. 59.

the three kingdoms of nature in our land.   In France his visits
to the museums and other establishments, with the inquiries of
Academicians and other men of science and letters respecting
this country, and their encomiums on the Philosophical Society
of Philadelphia, suggested to him the idea of engaging his native
State to do something in the same good but neglected cause."*

The Academy, from the first, was devoted chiefly to the physical sciences, and the papers in its memoirs for the most part
relate to astronomy and meteorology.

Among its early members I find the names of but two naturalists : The Rev. Manasseh Cutler, pastor of Ipswich Hamlet, one
of the earliest botanists of New England,† and William Dan-
dridge Peck [b. 1763, d. 1882], the author of the first paper on
systematic zoölogy ever published in America, a " Description
of four remarkable fishes, taken near the Piscataqua in New
Hampshire," published in 1794.‡   Peck, after graduating at
Harvard, lived at Kittery, N. H., and first became interested in
natural history by reading a wave-worn copy of Linné's " System of Nature," which he obtained from the ship which was
wrecked near his house.   He became a good entomologist, and
communicated much valuable material to Kirby in England, and
was also one of our first writers on the fungi.   He was the first
to occupy the chair of natural history in Harvard University, to
which he was appointed in 1800.

The Rev. Dr. Jedediah Morse [b. 1761, grad. Yale, 1783,
d. 1826] was the earliest of American geographers, and appears,
especially in the later gazetteers published by him, to have printed
important facts concerning the number and geographical distribution of the various Indian tribes.

The Connecticut Academy of Arts and Sciences was founded

* KIRTLAND: Mem. Amer. Acad.   New Series, vol. i, p. xxii.
† See previous address, p. 95.
‡ Mem. Amer. Acad. Sci., ii, Part ii, p. 46.   1797.

in 1799, one of the chief promoters being President Dwight [b. 1752, d. 1817], whose "Travels in New England and New York," printed in 1821, abounds with scientific observations. Another was E. C. Herrick [b. 1811, d. 1862], for many years librarian and subsequently treasurer of Yale College, whose observations upon the aurora, made in the latter years of the last century, are still frequently quoted; and later an active investigator of volcanic phenomena, and the author of a treatise on the Hessian fly and its parasites, the results of nine years' study; and of another on the existence of a planet between Mercury and the sun.

Benjamin Silliman [b. in Trumbull, Conn., Aug. 8, 1779, d. in New Haven, Nov. 27, 1869], who, in 1802, became Professor of Chemistry at Yale, began there his career of usefulness as an organizer, teacher, and critic. One of his introductions to popular favor was the paper which he, in conjunction with Prof. Kingsley, published, "An account of the meteor which burst over Weston, in Connecticut, in December, 1807." This paper attracted attention everywhere, for the nature of meteors was not well understood in those days. Jefferson was reputed to have said in reference to it, "that it was easier to believe that two Yankee professors could lie than to admit that stones could fall from heaven;" but I think this must be pigeon-holed with the millions of other slanders to which Jefferson was subjected in those days. I find in the papers by Rittenhouse and Madison, published twenty years before, by the Philosophical Society, matter-of-fact allusions to the falling of meteors to the earth.

Silliman was the earliest of American scientific lecturers who appeared before popular audiences, and, as founder and editor of the Journal of Science, did a service to science, the value of which is beyond estimate or computation.

Benjamin Waterhouse, Professor of the Theory and Practice of Medicine in Harvard, 1783-1812, was one of the earliest teachers of natural botany in America, and the author of a poem entitled " The Botanist." * The Rev. Jeremy Belknap [b. 1744, d. 1798], in his " History of New Hampshire," and the Rev. Samuel Williams [b. 1743, d. 1817], in his " Natural and Civil History of Vermont,"† made contributions to local natural history, and Capt. Jonathan Carver [b. 1732, d. 1780], in his " Travels through the Interior Parts of America," ‡ gave some meagre information as to the zoölogy and botany of regions previously unknown.

In the South the prestige of colonial days seemed to have departed. Except Jefferson, the only naturalist in Virginia was Dr. James Greenway, of Dinwiddie Co., a botanist of some merit. Mitchell returned to England before the Revolution, and Garden followed in 1784. H. B. Latrobe, of Baltimore, was an amateur ichthyologist, and Dr. James MacBride, of Pineville, S. C. [b. 1784, d. 1817], was an active botanist. Dr. Lionel Chalmers [b. 1715, d. 1777], who was for many years the leader of scientific activity in South Carolina, was omitted in the previous address. A graduate of Edinburgh, he was for forty years a physician in Charleston. He recorded observations on meteorology from 1750 to 1760, the foundation of his " Treatise on the Weather and Diseases of South Carolina " [London, 1776], and published also valuable papers on pathology. He was the host and patron of many naturalists, such as the Bartrams.

There was no lack of men in the South who were capable of appreciating scientific work. Virginia had fourteen members in the American Philosophical Society from 1780 to 1800, while Massachusetts and New York had only six each, the Carolinas had eight, and Maryland six. The population of the South was, however, widely dispersed and no concentration of effort

---

* Biography in Polyanthus, vol. ii.
† Walpole, N. H., 1794, 8vo, p. 416.
‡ 1778.

was possible. To this was due, no doubt, the speedy dissolution of the Academy of Arts and Sciences founded in Richmond in 1788.*

A name which should, perhaps, be mentioned in connection with this is that of Dr. William Charles Wells, whom it has been the fashion of late to claim as an American. It would be gratifying to be able to vindicate this claim, for Wells was a man of whom any nation might be proud. He was the originator of the generally-accepted theory of the origin of dew, and was also, as Darwin has shown, the first to recognize and announce the theory of evolution by natural selection.† Unfortunately Wells's science was not American science. We might with equal propriety claim as American the art of James Whistler, the politics of Parnell, the fiction of Alexandre Dumas, the essays of Grant Allen, or the science of Rumford and Le Vaillant.

Wells was the son of an English painter, who emigrated, in 1753, to South Carolina, where he remained until the time of the Revolution, when, with other loyalists, he returned to England. He was born during his father's residence in Charleston, but left the country in his minority ; was educated at Edinburgh, and though he, as a young physician, spent four years in the United States, he was permanently established in London practice fully twenty-eight years before he read his famous letter before the Royal Society.

The first American naturalist who held definite views as to evolution was, undoubtedly, Rafinesque.   In a letter to Dr. Torrey, Dec. 1, 1832, he wrote:

" The truth is that species, and perhaps genera also, are forming in organized beings by gradual deviations of shapes, forms, and organs taking place in the lapse of time.   There is a tendency

* See previous discourse, p. 98.
† DARWIN: Origin of species, 6th Amer. Ed., p xv. MORSE: Proc. Amer. Assoc. Adv. Science, xxv, p. 141.

to deviation and mutation in plants and animals by gradual steps, at remote, irregular periods. This is a part of the great universal law of *perpetual mutability* in everything."

It is pleasant to remember that both Darwin and Wallace owed much of their insight into the processes of nature to their American explorations. It is also interesting to recall the closing lines, almost prophetic as they seem to-day, of the "Epistle to the Author of the Botanic Garden," * written in 1798 by Elihu Hubbard Smith, of New York, and prefixed to the American editions of " The Botanic Garden :"

> " Where Mississippi's turbid waters glide
> And white Missouri pours its rapid tide ;
> Where vast Superior spreads its inland sea
> And the pale tribes near icy empires sway ;
> Where now Alaska lifts its forests rude
> And Nootka rolls her solitary flood.
> Hence keen incitement prompt the prying mind
> By treacherous fears, nor palsied nor confined ;
> Its curious search embrace the sea and shore
> And mine and ocean, earth and air explore.

> " Thus shall the years proceed,--till growing time
> Unfold the treasures of each different clime ;
> Till one vast brotherhood mankind unite
> In equal bonds of knowledge and of right ;
> Thus the proud column, to the smiling skies
> In simple majesty sublime shall rise,
> O'er ignorance foiled, their triumph loud proclaim,
> And bear inscribed, immortal, DARWIN's name."

XII.

During the three decades which made up the post-revolutionary period there were several " beginnings " which may not well be referred to in connection with individuals or localities.

The first book upon American insects was published in 1797, a sumptuously-illustrated work, in two volumes, with 104 colored plates, entitled " The Natural History of the rarer Lepidopterous Insects of Georgia." This was compiled by Sir James E. Smith from the notes and drawings of John Abbot

---

* **Erasmus**, grandfather of Charles Darwin.

[b. about 1760], living in England in 1840, an accomplished collector and artist, who had been for several years a resident of Georgia, gathering insects for sale in Europe. Mr. Scudder characterizes him as " the most prominent student of the life histories of insects we have ever had."*

There had, however, been creditable work previously done in what our entomologists are pleased to call the biological side of the science. As early as 1768, Col. Landon Carter, of " Sabine Hall," Virginia, prepared an elaborate paper " On the Habits of the Fly-Weevil that destroys the Wheat," which was printed by the American Philosophical Society,† accompanied by an extended report by " The Committee of Husbandry." In the same year Moses Bartram presented his " Observations on the native Silk-Worms of North America."‡

Organized effort in economic entomology appears to date from the year 1792, when the American Philosophical Society appointed a committee to collect materials for a natural history of the Hessian Fly, at that time making frightful ravages in the wheat-fields, and so much dreaded in Great Britain that the import of wheat from the United States was forbidden by law. The Philosophical Society's committee was composed of Thomas Jefferson, at that time Secretary of State in President Washington's cabinet, Benjamin Smith Barton, James Hutchinson, and Caspar Wistar. In their report, which was accompanied by large drawings, the history of the little marauder was given in considerable detail.

The publication of Wilson's American Ornithology, beginning in 1808, was an event of great importance. It was in 1804

*There is a whole series of quarto or folio volumes in the British Museum done by him, and a few volumes are extant in this country. Besides, all the biological material ,in Smith-Abbot's Insects of Georgia is his."—*Letter of S. H. Scudder.*

† Transactions of the American Philosophical Soc., 1, 274.

‡ *Ibid.*, p. 294.

that the author, a schoolmaster near Philadelphia, decided upon his plan. In a letter to Lawson he wrote:

"I am most earnestly bent on pursuing my plan of making a Collection of all the Birds of North America. Now, I don't want you to throw cold water on this notice, Quixotic as it may appear. I have been so long accustomed to the building of Airy Castles and brain Windmills that it has become one of my comforts of life, a sort of rough Bone, that amuses me when sated with the dull drudgery of Life."

I need not eulogize Wilson. Every one knows how well he succeeded. He has had learned commentators and eloquent biographers. Our children pore over the narrative of the adventurous life of the weaver naturalist, and we all are sensible of the charms which his graceful pen has given to the life-histories of the birds.

His poetical productions are immortal, and his lines to the Blue Bird and the Fisherman's Hymn are worthy to stand by the side of Bryant's Waterfowl, Trowbridge's Wood Pewee, Emerson's Titmouse, Thaxter's Sandpiper, and, possibly best of all, Walt. Whitman's Mocking-Bird in "Out of the Cradle endlessly Rocking."

Ichthyology in America dates also from these last years of the century. Garden was our only resident ichthyologist until Peck and Mitchill began their work, but Schœpf, the Hessian military surgeon, printed a paper on the Fishes of New York in 1787, and William Bryant, of New Jersey, and Henry Collins Flagg, of South Carolina, made observations upon the electric eel, in addition to those which Williamson, of North Carolina, laid before the Royal Society in 1775.

Paleontology had its beginning at about the same time in the publication of Jefferson's paper on the Megalonyx or "Great Claw" in 1797.*

---

* The first vertebrate fossils were found in Virginia. Samuel Maverick, of Massachusetts, reported to the colony at Boston in 1836 that, at a place

This early study of a fossil vertebrate was followed 20 years later by the first paper which touched upon invertebrates—that by Say on " Fossil Zoölogy," in the first volume of Silliman's Journal. Lesueur seems to have brought from France some knowledge of the names of fossils, and identified many species for the early American geologists.

Stratigraphical and physical geology also came in at this time, and will be referred to later.

The science of mineralogy was brought to America in its infancy. The first course of lectures upon this subject ever given in London was in the winter of 1793–4, by Schmeisser, a pupil of Werner. Dr. David Hosack, then a student of medicine at Edinburgh, was one of his hearers, and inspired by his enthusiasm began at once to form the collection of minerals which he brought to America on his return in 1794, which was the first mineralogical cabinet ever seen on this side of the Atlantic. This collection was exhibited for many years in New York (and in 1821 was given to Princeton College). Howard soon after obtained a select cabinet from Europe, and the museum of the American Philosophical Society acquired the Smith collection. In 1802, Mr. B. D. Perkins, a New York bookseller, brought from London a fine collection, which soon passed into the possession of Yale College, and in 1803 Dr. Archibald Bruce brought over one equally fine, which was made the basis of lectures. when in 1806 he became professor of mineralogy in Columbia College. George Gibbs, in 1805, imported the magnificent collection which was long in the custody of the American Geological Society. Seybert, about the same time, brought to Philadelphia the cabinet which in 1813 was bought by the Academy of Natural Sciences and was lectured upon by Troost in 1814.

---

on the James River, about sixty miles above its mouth, the colonists had found shells and bones, among these bones that of a whale, eighteen feet below the surface.—Neill's *Virginia Carolorum*, p. 131.

Much of the early botanical exploration was, however, carried out by European botanists : André Michaux [b. near Versailles, 1746, d. Madagascar, 1802], a pupil of the Jussiens and an experienced explorer, was sent by this government, in 1785, to collect useful trees and shrubs for naturalization in France. He remained eleven years; made extensive explorations in the regions then accessible, and as far west as the Mississippi ; sent home immense numbers of living plants ; and, after his return, in 1796, published his treatise on the American Oaks,* and prepared the materials for his posthumous " Flora Boreali-Americanas."

François André Michaux [b. near Versailles, 1770, d. at Vauréal, 1855] was his father's assistant in these early travels, and in 1802 and 1806 himself made botanical explorations in the Mississippi Valley. His botanical works were of great importance,† especially that known in its English translation as the " North American Sylva," afterward completed by Nuttall, and still the only work of the kind, though soon to be supplemented, we hope, by Professor Sargent's projected monographs.

Frederick Pursh [b. 1774, in Tobolsk, Siberia, d. June 11, 1820, in Montreal, Canada] carried on botanical explorations between 1799 and 1819 ; living, from 1802 to 1805, in Philadelphia, and from 1807 to 1810 in New York. In 1814 he published in London his " Flora Americæ Septemtrionalis." Pursh's Flora was largely based upon the labors of the American botanists Barton, Hosack, LeConte, Peck, Clayton, Walter, and Lyon, and the botanical collection of Lewis and Clarke, and enumerated about 3,000 species of plants, while Michaux's, printed eleven years before, had only about half that number.

A. von Enslen collected plants at this time, in the South and West, for the Imperial Cabinet in Vienna. C. C. Robin, who

---

* Histoire des chênes de l'Amerique Septentrionale, 1801 ; 36 plates.
† Voyage à l'ouest des monte Alléghany, &c. 8vo, pp. 684.   Paris, 1808,
‡Histoire des arbres foréstières de l'Amerique, Septentrionale,

travelled from 1802 to 1806 in what are now the Gulf States, wrote a botanical appendix to his Travels, published in 1807, on which Rafinesque founded his " Florula Ludoviciana " (New York, 1817).

Thaddeus Hænke [b. 1761, d. in Cochabamba, Bolivia, 1817] visited Western North America with the Spaniards late in the last century, and made large collections of plants, which were sent to the National Museum of Bohemia, at Prague, and in part described in Presl's " Reliquiæ Hænkianæ," 72 plates.

Archibald Menzies [b. 1754, d. 1842], an English naval surgeon, also collected on our Pacific coast, under Vancouver, in 1780–95, and his plants found their way to Edinburgh and Kew.

Captain Wangenheim, Surgeon Schoepf, of the Hessian contingent of the British army, Olaf Swartz, a Swedish botanical explorer, and others, also gathered plants in these early days, and, in some instances, published in Europe their botanical observations.

Other collectors of this same class were L. A. G. Bosc [1759–1828], who made botanical researches in the Carolinas during the last two years of the century, and returned to France in 1800 with a herbarium of 1,600 species. He also collected fishes, and his name is perpetuated in connection with at least two well-known American fauna. Another was M. Milbert, who collected for Cuvier in New York, Canada, the Great Lake region, and the Mississippi Valley from 1817 to 1823.

The Baron Palisot de Beauvois [b. 1755, d. 1820] came from Santo Domingo to America in 1791. He travelled extensively, and being a zoölogist as well as a botanist, made observations upon our native animals, particularly the reptiles.

It is to him that we owe the most carefully recorded of existing observations of young rattlesnakes crawling down their parent snakes' throats for protection from enemies.

Most of these men did not contribute largely to the advancement of American scientific institutes or affiliate with the naturalists of the day.

Of quite another type was the Count Luigi Castiglioni, who travelled, soon after the Revolution, throughout the Eastern States, and published in 1790 two volumes of his travels.*

The Count Volney [b. at Craon Feb. 3, 1757, d. in Paris April 25, 1820], traveller, statesman, and historian, travelled in this country from 1795 to 1798, and in 1803, while a Senator of the French Republic, published his famous work upon the United States, containing his observations upon its soil and its climate, and upon the Indians, together with the first doctrines of the language of the Miamis,† and also giving a description of the physical and botanical features of the country. Volney was an admirer and intimate friend of Franklin, and it was in his home at Passy, we are told, that he conceived the idea of his most famous book "Les Ruines."‡

Among the traditions of Fauquier county, Virginia, is one which is of interest to naturalists, since it relates to an incident showing the interest of our first President in science :

"About the year 1796," runs the story, "at the close of a long summer's day, a stranger entered the village of Warrenton. He was alone, and on foot, and his appearance was anything but prepossessing. His garments, coarse and dust-covered, indicated an individual in the humble walks. From a cane across his shoulders was suspended a handkerchief containing his clothing. Stopping in front of Turner's tavern, he took from his hat a paper and handed it to a gentleman standing on the steps ; it read as follows :

"The celebrated historian and naturalist
VOLNEY needs no recommendation from
"G. WASHINGTON."

---

* Viaggio negli Stati Uniti del America Settentrionali.

† Tableau du climat et du sol des Etats-Unis d'Amerique, suivi d'eclaircissements sur la Floride, sur la colonie française a Scioto sur quelques colonies canadiennes, et sur les savages. Paris, 1803. 8vo, 2 vols. 2d edition. Paris. 8vo, 1 vol., pp. 494. Map.

‡ BIGELOW, JOHN : Franklin's Home and Host. in France. *The Century*, May, 1888, p. 743.

In 1801 Jefferson began his eight years of presidency. Since he was the only man of science who has ever occupied the chief magistracy, he has a right to a high place in the esteem of such a society as ours, and I only regret that, having spoken of him at length a year ago, I cannot now discuss his scientific career in all its aspects.

I then spoke of the credit which was due to him for beginning so early as 1780 to agitate the idea of a government exploring expedition to the Pacific, which culminated in the sending out by Congress of the expedition of Lewis and Clarke, in 1803. Captain Lewis [b. 1774, d. 1809], the leader of this expedition, was a young Virginian, the neighbor, and for some years the private secretary, of President Jefferson. He set out in the summer of 1803, accompanied by his associate, Captain Clarke, and twenty-eight men. They entered the Missouri, May 14, 1804, before the middle of the following July had reached the great falls, and by October were upon the western slope, where, embarking in canoes upon the Kouskousky, a branch of the Columbia, they descended to its mouth, where they arrived on the 15th of November, 1805. The following spring they retraced their course, arriving at St. Louis in September.* The results of the expedition were first made known in Jefferson's message to Congress, read February 19, 1806.

The statue of Meriwether Lewis is one of those at the base of the Washington Monument in Richmond, Virginia, and is worthy of the man and his career.

Dr. Asa Gray in a recent letter says:

" I have reason to think that Michaux suggested to Jefferson the expedition which the latter was active in sending over to the Pacific. I wonder if he put off Michaux for the sake of having it in American hands?"†

The idea of an expedition to the Pacific was one which was likely

---

* See a complete bibliography of the various reports of this expedition, by Elliott Coues, in the Bulletin of the U. S. Geological Survey.

† See Amer. Journ. Sci., xii, No. 1.

to occur to any thoughtful American, and was, after all, simply the continuing of a plan as old as the Spanish days of discovery. Jefferson, at all events, was an active promoter of all such enterprises, and after a quarter of a century's effort the expedition was dispatched, while in 1805 Gen. Z. M. Pike was sent to explore the sources of the Mississippi river and the western parts of " Louisiana," penetrating as far west as " Pike's Peak," a name which still remains as a memento of this enterprise.

The organization of these early expeditions marked the beginning of one of the most important portions of the scientific work of our government—the investigation of the resources and natural history of the public domain. The expeditions of Lewis and Clarke, and of Pike, were the precursors and prototypes of the magnificent organization now accomplishing so much for science under the charge of Major J. W. Powell.

As early as 1806, Jefferson, inspired by Patterson and Hassler, urged the establishment of a national Coast Survey, and in this was earnestly supported by his Secretary of the Treasury, Albert Gallatin, who drew up a learned and elaborate project for its organization, and an act authorizing its establishment was passed in 1807. During his administration, in 1802, the first scientific school in this country was established, the Military Academy at West Point. The Military Academy was a favorite project of General Washington, who is said to have justified his anxiety for its establishment by the remark that " an army of asses led by a lion is vastly superior to an army of lions led by an ass."

Jefferson has been heartily abused for not gratifying Alexander Wilson's request to be appointed naturalist to Pike's expeditions. It is possible that even in those days administrators were hampered by lack of financial resources. It must also be remembered that in 1804 Wilson was simply an enthusiastic projector of ornithological undertakings, and had done nothing whatever to establish his reputation as an investigator.

One of Jefferson's first official acts was to throw his presidential mantle over Priestley.   Two weeks after he became President of the United States he wrote these words:

"It is with heartfelt satisfaction that, in the first moments of my public action, I can hail you with welcome to our land, tender to you the homage of its respect and esteem, cover you under the protection of those laws which were made for the wise and good like you, and disclaim the legitimacy of that libel on legislators which, under the form of a law, was for some time placed among them."
* * * "Yours is one of the few lives precious to mankind, and for the continuance of which every thinking man is solicitous. Bigots may be an exception.   What an effort, my dear sir, of bigotry in politics and religion have we gone through. * * * All advances in science were prescribed as innovations.   They pretended to praise and encourage education, but it was to be the education of our ancestors.   We were to look backwards, not forwards for improvement; the President (Washington) himself declaring in one of his answers to addresses that we were never to expect to go beyond them in real science.   This was the real ground of all the attacks on you; those who live by mystery and *charlatanerie* fearing you would render them useless by simplifying the Christian philosophy, the most sublime and benevolent, but most perverted system that ever shone on man, endeavored to crush your well-earned and well-deserved fame."*

XIII.

With the close of the third decade ended the first third of a century since the Declaration of Independence.   We have now passed in review a considerable number of illustrious names and have noted the inception of many worthy undertakings.

"Still, however," in the words of Silliman, "although individuals were enlightened, no serious impression was produced on the public mind; a few lights were, indeed, held out, but they were lights twinkling in an almost impervious gloom."†

This was a state of affairs not peculiar to America.   A gloom no less oppressive had long obscured the intellectual atmosphere

---

* Jefferson's Works (T. J. Randolph ed.), 1830, iii, 461.
† Silliman, i, 37.

of the old world. There were a goodly number of men of science, and many important discoveries were being made, but no bonds had yet been formed to connect the interests of the men of science and the men of affairs.

Speculative science, in the nature of things, can only interest and attract scholarly men. and though its results, concisely and attractively stated, may have a passing interest to a certain portion of every community, it is only by its practical applications that it secures the hearty support of the community at large.

Huxley, in his recent discourse upon " The Advance of Science in the Last Half Century,"* has touched upon this subject in a most suggestive and instructive manner, and has shown that Bacon, with all his wisdom, exerted little direct beneficial influence upon the advancement of natural knowledge, which has after all been chiefly forwarded by men like Galileo and Harvey, Boyle and Newton, "who would have done their work quite as well if neither Bacon nor Descartes had ever propounded their views respecting the manner in which scientific investigation should be pursued."

I think we should look upon Bacon as the prophet of modern scientific thought, rather than its founder. It is no doubt true, as Huxley has said, that his " scientific insight " was not sufficient to enable him to shape the future course of scientific philosophy, but it is scarcely true that he attached any undue value to the practical advantages which the world as a whole, and incidentally science itself, were to reap from the applications of scientific methods to the investigation of nature.

Even though the investigations of Descartes, Newton, Leibnitz, Boyle, Torricelli, and Malpighi, had directly helped no man to either wealth or comfort, the cumulative results of their labors, and those of their pupils and associates, resulted in a condition

---

* WOOD, T. H. : The Reign of Victoria; a survey of Fifty Years of Progress. London, 1887.

of scientific knowledge from which, sooner or later, utilitarian results must necessarily have sprung.

It is true, as Huxley tells us, that at the beginning of this century weaving and spinning were still carried on with the old appliances ; true that nobody could travel faster by sea or by land than at any previous time in the world's history, and true that King George could send a message from London to York no faster than King John might have done. Metals were still worked from their ores by immemorial rule of thumb, and the centre of the iron trade of these islands was among the oak forests of Sussex, while the utmost skill of the British mechanic did not get beyond the production of a coarse watch.

It cannot be denied that although the middle of the eighteenth century was illuminated by a host of great names in science, chemists, biologists, geologists, English, French, German, and Italian, the deepening and broadening of natural knowledge had produced next to no immediate practical benefits. Still I cannot believe that Bacon, the prophet, would have been so devoid of " scientific insight" as to have failed to foresee at this time the ultimate results of all this intellectual activity.

But Huxley says :

" Even if, at this time, Francis Bacon could have returned to the scene of his greatness and of his littleness, he must have regarded the philosophic world which praised and disregarded his precepts with great disfavor. If ghosts are consistent, he would have said, " these people are all wasting their time, just as Gilbert, and Kepler, and Galileo, and my worthy physician Harvey did in my day. Where are the fruits of the restoration of science which I promised? This accumulation of bare knowledge is all very well, but *cui bono?* Not one of these people is doing what I told him specially to do, and seeking that secret of the cause of forms, which will enable him to deal at will with matter and superinduce new nature upon old foundations."

As Huxley, however, proceeds himself to show, in the discussion which immediately follows this passage, a " new nature, begotten by science upon fact," has been born within the past few decades, and pressing itself daily and hourly upon our attention, has worked miracles which have not only modified the whole future of the lives of mankind, but has reacted constantly upon the progress of science itself.

It is to the development of this new nature, then in its very infancy, that we must look for the revival of interest in science on this side of the Atlantic.

The second decade of the century was marked by a great accession of interest in the sciences. The second war with Great Britain having ended, the country, for the first time since colonial days, became sufficiently tranquil for peaceful attention to literature and philosophy. The end of the Napoleonic wars and the restoration of tranquillity to Europe tended to scientific advances on the other side of the Atlantic, and the results of the labors of Cuvier, whose glory was now approaching its zenith, of Brongniart, of Blainville, of Jussieu, of Decandolle, of Werner, of Hutton, of Buckland, of De la Beche, of Magendie, of Humboldt, Daubuisson, Berzelius, Von Buch, of Herschel, of Laplace, of Young, of Fresnel, of Oersted, of Cavendish, of Lavoisier, Wollaston, Davy, and Sir William Hooker, were eagerly welcomed by hundreds in America.

" In truth," wrote one who was among the most active in promoting these tendencies, " in truth, a thirst for the Natural Sciences seemed already to pervade the United States like the progress of an epidemic."

The author of these enthusiastic words was Amos Eaton [b. in Chatham, N. Y., 1776, d. May 6, 1842], one of the most interesting men of his day. In 1816, at the age of forty, he abandoned the practice of law and went to New Haven to attend Silliman's lectures on Mineralogy and Geology. He was a man of great force and untiring energy, and one of the pioneers of American geology ; though the name, " father of American geology," sometimes applied to him, would seem to belong more appropriately to Maclure, or, perhaps, to Mitchill. He was, however, only some eight years later than Maclure in beginning geological field-work. Eaton's "Index to the Geology of the Northern States of America," printed in 1817, was the first strictly American treatise, and seems to have had a very stimulating effect. He was pre-eminently an agitator and an educator. He travelled many thousands of miles on foot throughout New England and New York, delivering, in the meantime, at the principal towns, short courses of lectures on natural history. In March, 1817, having received an invitation to aid in the introduction of the Natural Sciences in Williams College, his Alma Mater, he delivered a course of lectures in Williamstown. "Such," he remarks, "was the zeal at this institution that an uncontrollable enthusiasm for natural history took possession of every mind; and other departments of learning were, for a time, crowded out of the college. The authorities allowed twelve students each day (seventy-two per week) to devote their whole time to the collection of minerals and plants, in lieu of all other exercises."*

In April, 1818, he went to Albany on the special invitation of Gov. DeWitt Clinton and delivered a course of lectures on Natural History. "In Albany I found," wrote he, "Dr. T. Romeyn Beck, and in Troy, Doctors Burrett, Robbins, and Dale, zealous beyond description in the cause of Natural Science. By the exertions of these gentlemen a taste for the study of Nature was strongly excited in those two cities, especially for that of geology. They, together with several others, had become members of the New York Lyceum of Natural History, and, in the fall of 1818, established a society of the same name and upon a similar plan in Troy. Collections were made with such zeal that, in the course of a few months, Troy could boast

---

* Geological Text-Book, 2d ed., 1832, p. 16.

of a more extensive collection of American geological specimens than Yale College, or any other institution upon this continent."*

" In this period," remarked Bache, " the prosecution of mathematics and physical science was neglected ; indeed barely kept alive by the calls for boundary and land surveys of the more extended class, by the exertions necessary in the lecture-room, or by isolated volunteer efforts.

"As the country was explored and settled the unworked mine of natural history was laid open, and the attention of almost all the cultivators of science was turned toward the development of its riches.

" Descriptive natural history is the pursuit which emphatically made that period. As its experiment may be taken the admirable descriptive mineralogy of Cleaveland, which seemed to fill the measures of that day and be, as it were, its chief embodiment, appearing just as the era was passing away."†

The leading spirits of the day seem to have been Silliman, Hare, Maclure, Mitchill, Gibbs, Cleaveland, DeWitt Clinton, and Caspar Wistar.

Names familiar to us of the present generation began now to appear in scientific literature : Isaac• Lea began to print his memoirs on the *Unionidæ;* Edward Hitchcock, principal of the Deerfield Academy, was writing his first papers on the geology of Massachusetts ; Prof. Chester Dewey, of Williams College, [b. 1781, d. 1867], afterwards known to us all from his excellent work upon the Carices, was discussing the mineralogy and geology of Massachusetts ; Dr. John Torrey, also to be famous as a botanist, was then devoting his attention to mineralogy and

---

* The Troy Lyceum of Natural History was incorporated in 1819, and a lectureship was created, filled by Mr. Eaton (*Silliman's Journal,* ii, 173). In 1820 a similar association, " The Hudson Association for Improvement in Science," was founded in the city of Hudson, and in 1821 the Delaware Chemical and Geological Society.

† Presidential Address Am. Assoc. Adv. Sci., 1851, pp. vi, xlvi.

chemistry; Dr. Jacob Porter was making botanical observations in central Massachusetts; quaint old Caleb Atwater, at that time almost the only scientific observer west of the Alleghanies, was discussing the origin of prairies, meteorology, botany, geology, mineralogy, and scenery of the Ohio country, and a little later the remains of mammoths.

Prof. J. W. Webster, of Boston, was making general studies in geology; the Rev. Elias Cornelius and Mr. John Grammer were writing of the geology of Virginia; Mr. J. A. Kain, upon that of Tennessee, I. P. Brace, that of Connecticut, and James Pierce, that of New Jersey.

To this period belonged the brilliant Constantine Rafinesque, with Torrey, Silliman, Cleaveland, Gibbs, James, Schoolcraft, Gage, Akerly, Mitchill, Dana, Beck, and Featherstonhaugh.

Dr. Henry R. Schoolcraft, afterwards prominent in ethnology, printed, in 1819, his "View of the Lead Mines of Missouri," the first from American contributors to economic geology; and in the same year his "Transallegania," a mineralogical poem, probably the last as well as the first of its kind written in America. In 1821 he published a scholarly "Account of the Native Copper on the Southern shore of Lake Superior."*

Mineralogy and geology were the most popular of the sciences.

American Geology dated its beginning from this previous decade. Prof. S. L. Mitchill was one of the first to call attention to the teachings of Kirwan and the pioneers of European geology, and very early in the century began to instruct the students of Columbia College in the principles of geology as then understood. He published Observations on the Geology of America, and also edited a New York edition of Cuvier's "History of the Earth," contributing to this work an appendix which was constantly quoted by early writers.

The first geological explorer was William Maclure [b. in Ayr,

---

* Amer. Jour. Science, iii, pp. 201-210.

Scotland, 1763, d. in San Angel, Mexico, Mar. 23, 1840], a Scotch merchant who amassed a large fortune by commercial connections with this country, and became a citizen of the United States about 1796. His most important service to American science was that of a patron, for he was a liberal supporter of the infant Academy of Sciences in Philadelphia, and for twenty-two years its president, besides being an upholder of other important enterprises.

The publication in 1809 of his "Observations on the Geology of the United States" marks the beginning of American geographical geology and the first attempt at a geological survey of the United States. This had long been the object of his ambition, and, in order to prepare himself for the task, he had spent several years in travel throughout Europe, making observations and collecting objects in natural history, which he forwarded to the country of his adoption.

His undertaking was undoubtedly a remarkable one. "He went forth with his hammer in his hand and his wallet on his shoulder, pursuing his researches in every direction, visiting almost every State and Territory, wandering often amidst pathless tracts and dreary solitudes until he had crossed and recrossed the Alleghany mountains not less than fifty times. He encountered all the privations of hunger, thirst, fatigue, and exposure, month after month and year after year, until his indomitable spirit had conquered every difficulty and crowned his enterprise with success,"* and after the publication of his memoir he devoted eight years more to collecting materials for a second and revised addition.

The geological map of the United States, published in 1809, appears to have been the first of the kind ever attempted for an entire country. Smith's geological map of England was six years later, and Greenough's still subsequent in date.

---

* MARTIN: Memoir of William Maclure, p. 11.

The publication in London in 1813 of Bakewell's "Introduction to Geology" seems to have given a great stimulus to geological researches in this country, as may be judged from the publication of an American edition a year or two later. Mitchill, Bruce, and Maclure soon had a goodly band of associates. Naturalists were not confined to limited specialties in those days, and we find all the chemists, botanists, and zoölogists absorbed in the consideration of geological problems. Maclure and most of the Americans were disciples of Werner. Silliman, writing in 1818, said:

"A grand outline has recently been drawn by Mr. Maclure with a masterly hand and with a vast extent of personal observation and labour; but, to fill up the detail, both observation and labour still more extensive are demanded; nor can the object be effected till more good geologists are formed and distributed over our extensive territory."

On the 6th of September, 1819, the American Geological Society was organized in the philosophical room of Yale College, an event of great importance in the history of science, hastening, as it seems to have done, the establishment of State surveys and stimulating observation throughout the country. This Society, which continued in existence until about 1826, may fairly be considered the nucleus of the Association of American Geologists and Naturalists, and, consequently, of the American Association for the Advancement of Science. Members appended to their names the symbols, M. A. G. S., and it was for a time the most active of American scientific societies.

The characteristics of the leading spirits were summed up by Eaton at the time of its beginning:

"The President, William Maclure, has already struck out the grand outline of North American geographical geology. The first Vice-President, Col. G. Gibbs, has collected more facts and amassed more geological and mineralogical specimens than any other individual of the age. The second Vice-President, Professor Silliman, gives the true scientific dress to all the naked mineralogical subjects which are furnished to his hand.   The third Vice-President, Professor Cleaveland, is successfully employed in elucidating and familiarizing those interesting scenes; and thus smoothing the rugged paths of the student.   Professor Mitchill has amassed a large store of materials and annexed them to the labors of Cuvier and Jameson.   The drudgery of climbing cliffs and descending into fissures and caverns, and of traversing in all directions our most rugged mountainous districts, to ascertain the distinctive characters, number, and order of our strata, has devolved upon me."*

Eaton has very fairly defined his own position among the early geologists, which was that of an explorer and pioneer.   The epithet, " Father of American Geology," which has sometimes been applied to him, might more justly be bestowed upon Maclure, or even upon Mitchill.   The name of Amos Eaton [b. 1776, d. 1872] will always be memorable, on account of his connection with the geological survey of New York, which was begun in 1820, at the private expense of Hon. Stephen Van Rensselaer; also as the founder, in 1824, of the Rensselaer Polytechnic Institute, the first of its class on the continent.

The State of New York was not pre-eminently prompt in establishing an official survey, but the liberality of Van Rensselaer and the energy of Eaton gave to New York the honor of attaching the names of its towns and counties to a large number of the geological formations of North America.

In these early surveys Eaton was associated with Dr. Theodore Romeyn Beck and Mr. H. Webster, naturalist and collector, one of the first being a survey of the county of Albany, under the special direction of a County Agricultural Society, followed by similar surveys of Rensselaer county and Saratoga county and others along the Erie Canal.

In July, 1818, Professor Silliman began the publication of the *American Journal of Science*, which has been for more than two-thirds of a century the most prominent register of the scien-

---

* Index to the Geology of the Northern States. 2d ed. 1820. p. viii.

tific progress of this continent. Silliman's journal succeeded, and far more than replaced, the *American Mineralogical Journal*, the earliest of American scientific periodicals, which was established in New York 1810 by Dr. Archibald Bruce, and which was discontinued after the close of the first volume, in 1814, on account of the illness and untimely death of its projector.* The *Mineralogical Journal* was not so limited in scope as in name, and was for a time the principal organ of our scientific specialists.†

We can but admire the spirit of Silliman, who remarks in the preface to the third volume:

" It must require several years from the commencement of the work to decide the question [whether it is to be supported], and the editor (if God continues his life and health) will endeavour to prove himself neither impatient nor querulous during the time that his countrymen hold the question undecided, *whether there shall be an American Journal of Science and Arts.*"

In the fall of 1822 he announced that a trial of four years had decided the point that the American public would support this journal.

Prior to the establishing of Silliman's journal, the principal organs of American science were the *Medical Repository*, commenced in 1798, of which Dr. Mitchill was the chief proprietor; the *New York Medical and Physical Journal*, conducted chiefly by Dr. Hosack; the *Boston Journal of Philosophy and the Arts*, and other similar periodicals. Our students looked chiefly, however, to the English journals— Tilloch's *Philosophical Magazine* and Nicholson's *Journal of Natural Philosophy*, and later, Thomson's *Annals of Philosophy*, the *Annales de Chimie*.

---

* "No future historian of American science will fail to commemorate this work us our earliest *purely scientific* journal, supported by *original American communications*," said Silliman in his prospectus, 1817.

† The only copies of this journal known to be in existence are in the N. Y. State Library and the Harvard Library.

The American Monthly Magazine, established in 1814 by Charles Brockden Brown, was fully as much devoted to science as to literature, and an examination of this and other journals of the early portion of the century will, I think, satisfy the student that scientific subjects were more seriously considered by our ancestors than by the Americans of to-day. *The American Monthly* published elaborate reviews of technical works, such as Cleaveland's Mineralogy, and summaries of the world's progress in science, as well as the monthly proceedings of all the scientific societies in New York, and papers on systematic zoölogy and botany by Rafinesque.

In 1812 the American Antiquarian Society was established at Worcester, and before 1820, when its first volume of transactions appeared, had collected 6,000 books and "a respectable cabinet." This was a pioneer effort in ethnological science. *Archæologia Americana* contained papers by Mitchill, Atwater, and others, chiefly relating to the aboriginal population of America. The name of Isaiah Thomas, LL. D. [b. in Boston 1749, d. in Worcester 1831], the founder and first president of the society, who at his own expense erected a building for its accommodation and endowed its first researches, should be remembered with gratitude by American naturalists. He was one of the most eminent of American printers, and styled by DeWarville "the Didot of America."

In 1812 the Academy of Natural Sciences of Philadelphia was founded, the outgrowth of a social club, whose members, we are told, had no conception of the importance of the work they were undertaking when, in a spirit of burlesque, they assumed the title of an academy of learning.

In 1816 the Coast Survey, after years of discussion, was placed in action under the supervision of Hassler (who had been appointed its head as early as 1811), but, two years later, the work going on too slowly to please the Government, it was stopped.

The Linnæan Society of New England, established in Boston about this time, was the precursor of the Boston Society of Natural Science.

The publication of an American edition of Rees's Cyclopædia, in Philadelphia, was begun in 1810, and the 47th volume completed in 1824. This was an event in the history of American science, for it furnished employment and thus fostered the investigations of several eminent naturalists, among whom were Alexander Wilson, Thomas Say, and Ord; while, at the same time, it fostered a taste for science in the United States and gave currency to several rather epoch-making articles, such as Say's upon Conchology and Entomology.

Mr. Bradbury, the publisher of this Cyclopædia, was the first of a goodly company of liberal and far-seeing publishers who have done much for science in this country by their patronage of important scientific publications.

In 1817 Josiah Meigs, Commissioner of the Land Office, issued a circular to the several Registers of the Land Offices of the United States requiring them to keep daily meteorological observations, and also to report upon such phenomena as the times of the unfolding of leaves of plants and the dates of flowering, the migrations of birds and fishes, the dates of spawning of fishes, the hibernation of animals, the history of locusts and other insects in large numbers, the falling of stones and other bodies from the atmosphere, the direction of meteors, and discoveries relative to the antiquities of the country.

It does not appear that anything ever resulted from this step, but it is referred to as an indication that, seventy years ago, our Government was willing to use its civil service officials in the interest of science. A few years later the same idea was carried into effect by the Smithsonian Institution.

In those early days each of the principal cities had public museums founded and supported by private enterprise. Their proprietors were men of scientific tastes, who affiliated with the naturalists of the day and placed their collections freely at the disposal of investigators.

The earliest was the Philadelphia Museum, established by Charles Wilson Peale, and for a time housed in the building of the American Philosophical Society. In 1800 it was full of popular attractions.

" There were a mammoth's tooth from the Ohio, and a woman's shoe from Canton ; nests of the kind used to make soup of, and a Chinese fan six feet long ; bits of asbestos, belts of wampum, stuffed birds and feathers from the Friendly Islands, scalps, tomahawks, and long lines of portraits of great men of the Revolutionary War. To visit the Museum, to wander through the rooms, play upon the organ, examine the rude electrical machine, and have a profile drawn by the physiognomitian, were pleasures from which no stranger to the city ever refrained."

Dr. Hare's oxyhydrogen blow-pipe was shown in this Museum by Mr. Rubens Peale as early as 1810.

The Baltimore Museum was managed by Rembrandt Peale, and was in existence as early as 1815 and as late as 1830.*

Earlier efforts were made, however, in Philadelphia. Dr. Chovet, of that city, had a collection of wax anatomical models made by him in Europe, and Prof. John Morgan, of the University of Pennsylvania, who learned his methods from the Hunters in London and Sué in Paris, was also forming such a collection before the Revolution.†

The Columbian Museum and Turrell's Museum, in Boston, are spoken of in the annals of the day, and there was a small collection in the attic of the State House in Hartford.

---

* " Baltimore has a handsome museum superintended by one of the Peale family, well known for their devotion to natural science and to works of art. It is not their fault if the specimens which they are enabled to display in the latter department are very inferior to their splendid exhibitions in the former."—Mrs. Trollope, *Domestic Manners of the Americans.* London, 1831.

† Trans. Amer. Phil. Soc., ii, p. 366.

The Western Museum, in Cincinnati, was founded about 1815, by Robert Best, M. D., afterwards of Lexington, Ky., who seems to have been a capable collector, and who contributed matter to Godman's " American Natural History." In 1818 a society styled the Western Museum Society was organized among the citizens, which, though scarcely a scientific organization, seems to have taken a somewhat liberal and public-spirited view of what a museum should be.   To the naturalist of to-day there is something refreshing in such simple appeals as the following:

" In collecting the fishes and reptiles of the Ohio the managers will need all the aid which their fellow-citizens may feel disposed to give them.   Although not a very interesting department of zoölogy, no object of the Society offers so great a prospect of novelty as that which embraces these animals.

" The obscure and neglected race of insects will not be overlooked, and any specimen sufficiently perfect to be introduced into a cabinet of entomology will be thankfully received."*

Major John Eatton LeConte, U. S. A. [b. 1784, d. 1860], was a very successful student of botany and zoölogy.   He published many botanical papers and contributions to descriptive zoölogy, and also in Paris, in conjunction with Boisduval, the first instalment of a work, of which he was really sole author, upon the Lepidoptera of North America.†

The elder brother, Dr. Lewis LeConte [b. 1782, d. 1838], was equally eminent as an observer, and was, for forty years, one of the most prominent naturalists in the South.   On his plantation in Liberty county, Ga., he established a botanical garden and a chemical laboratory.   His zoölogical manuscripts were destroyed in the burning of Columbia just at the close of the civil war, but his observations, which he was averse to publishing in his own name, were, we are told, embodied in the writings of his

---

*An Address to the people of the Western Country, dated Cincinnati, Sept. 15, 1818, and signed by Elijah Slack, James Findlay, William Steele, Jesse Embrees, and Daniel Drake, Managers.

† Histoire Generale et Iconographie.

brother, of Stephen Elliott, of the Scotch botanist Gordon,* of Dr. William Baldwin, and others.† ‡

Stephen Elliott, of Charleston, South Carolina [b. 1711, d. 1830], was a graduate of Yale in the class of 1791, and, while prominent in the political and financial circles of his State, found time to cultivate science. He founded in 1813 the Literary and Philosophical Society of South Carolina, and was its first president; and in 1829 was elected Professor of Natural History and Botany in the South Carolina Medical College, which he aided to establish. He published " The Botany of South Carolina and Georgia " (Charleston, 1821–27), having been assisted in its preparation by Dr. James McBride; and had an extensive museum of his own gathering. The Elliott Society of Natural History, founded in 1853, or before, and subsequently continued under the name of the Elliott Society of Science and Art, 1859–75, was named in memory of this public-spirited man.

Jacob Green [b. 1790, d. 1841], at different times professor in the College of New Jersey and in Jefferson Medical College, was one of the old school naturalists, equally at home in all of the sciences. His paper on Trilobites (1832) was our first formal contribution to invertebrate paleontology; his "Account of some new species of Salamanders,"§ one of the earliest steps in American herpetology; his " Remarks on the Unios of the United States,"‖ the beginning of studies subsequently extensively prosecuted by Lea and some other entomologists. He also wrote upon the crystallization of snow, and was the author of " Chemical

---

* Loudon's Gardeners' Magazine.

† A. H. Stephens in *Johnson's Cyclopædia*, p. 1702.

‡ The LeConte family deserves a place in Galto's " Hereditary Genius." Prof. John LeConte, the physicist, and Prof. Joseph LeConte, the geologist, were sons of Dr. Lewis LeConte; while Dr. J. L. LeConte is the son of his brother, Major LeConte.

§ Contributions of the Maclurian Lyceum, i, Jan., 1827, p. 3.

‖ Ibid, i, ii, 41.

Philosophy," "Astronomical Researches," and a work upon Botany of the United States.

The earlier volumes of Silliman's Journal were filled with notes of his observations in all departments of natural history.

José Francisco Correa da Serra, secretary of the Royal Academy of Lisbon, was resident in Philadelphia in 1813, in the capacity of Portuguese minister, and affiliated with our men of science in botanical and geological interests. In 1814 he lectured on botany in the place of B. S. Barton, and also published several botanical papers, as well as one upon the soil of Kentucky.

Alire Raffenau Delile, formerly a member of Napoleon's scientific expedition to Egypt, and the editor of the "Flora of Egypt," was in New York about this time, for the purpose of completing his medical education, and seems to have done much to stimulate interest in botanical studies.

To this as well as to the subsequent period belonged Dr. Gerard Troost [b. in Holland, Mar. 15, 1776, ed. at Leyden, d. at Nashville, Aug. 17, 1850], a naturalist of Dutch birth and education, who came to Philadelphia in 1810, and was a founder and the first President of the Philadelphia Academy. In 1826 he founded a Geological Survey of the environs of Philadelphia; in 1827 became Professor of Chemistry, Mineralogy and Geology in the University of Nashville. As State geologist of Tennessee from 1831–49 he published some of the earliest State geological reports.

Another expedition, well worthy of mention, though not exceedingly fruitful, was one made under the direction of Mr. Maclure, President of the Philadelphia Academy, to the Sea Islands of Georgia and the Florida peninsula. The party consisted of Maclure, Say, Ord, and Titian R. Peale, and its results, though not embodied in a formal report, may be detected in the scientific literature of the succeeding years. This was early in 1818, while Florida was still under the dominion of

Spain, and the expedition was finally abandoned, owing to the hostile attitude of the Seminole Indians in that territory.

XIV.

The third decade of the century, beginning with 1820, was marked by a continuation of the activities of that which pre-ceeded. In 1826 there were in existence twenty-five scientific societies, more than half of them especially devoted to natural history,* and nearly all of very recent origin.

The leading spirits were Mitchill, Maclure, Webster, Torrey, Silliman, Gibbs, LeConte,. Dewey, Hare, Hitchcock, Olmstead, Eliot, and T. R. Beck.

Nathaniel Bowditch [b. 1773, d. 1838], who, in 1829, began the publication of his magnificent translation of the "Mecanique Celeste" of La Place, with those scholarly commentations which secured him so lofty a place among the mathematicians of the world.

Still more important was the lesson of his noble devotion of his life and fortune to science. The greater part of his monu-mental work was completed, we are told, in 1817, but he found that to print it would cost $12,000, a sum far beyond his means. A few years later, however, he began its publication from his own limited means, and the work was continued, after his death, by his wife. The dedication is to his wife, and tells us that " without her approbation the work would not have been under-taken."

Another person was W. C. Redfield [b. 1789, d. 1857], who, in 1827, promulgated the essential portions of the theory of storms, which is now pretty generally accepted, and which was subsequently extended by Sir William Reid in Barbadoes and Bermuda, and greatly modified by Professor Loomis, of New Haven. An eloquent eulogy of Redfield was pronounced by

---

* Amer. Journ. Sci., x, p. 368. (Cut).

Professor Denison Olmsted at the Montreal meeting of the American Association in 1857.*

Among the rising young investigators appear the names of Joseph Henry, A. D. Bache, C. U. Shepard, the younger Silliman, Henry Seybert, William Mather, Ebenezer Emmons, Percival, the poet geologist, DeKay, Godman, and Harlan.

The organization, in 1824, of the Rensselaer School, afterwards the Rensselaer Polytechnic Institute, at Troy, marked the beginning of a new era in scientific and technological education. Its principal professors were Amos Eaton and Dr. Lewis C. Beck.

In 1820 an expedition was sent by the General Government to explore the Northwestern Territory, especially the region around the Great Lakes and the sources of the Mississippi. This was under charge of Gen. Lewis Cass, at that time Governor of Michigan Territory. Henry R. Schoolcraft accompanied this expedition as mineralogist, and Capt. D. B. Douglass, U. S. A., as topographical engineer ; and both of these sent home considerable collections reported upon by the specialists of the day. Cass himself, though better known as a statesman, was a man of scientific tastes and ability, and his " Inquiries respecting the History, Traditions, Languages, &c., of the Indians," published at Detroit in 1823, is a work of high merit.

Long's expeditions into the far West were also in progress at this time, under the direction of the General Government; the first, or Rocky Mountain, exploration in 1819–20; the second to the sources of the St. Peter's, in 1823. In the first expedition Major Long was accompanied by Edwin James as botanist and geologist, who also wrote the Narrative published in 1823. The second expedition was accompanied by William H. Keating, Professor of Mineralogy and Chemistry in the University of Pennsylvania, who was its geologist and historiographer. Say

---

* See History of N. Y. Academy of Science, p. 76.

was the zoölogist of both explorations. De Schweinitz worked
up the botanical material which he collected.

The English expeditions sent to Arctic North America under
the command of Sir John Franklin were also out during these
years, the first from 1819 to 1822, the second from 1825 to 1827,
and yielded many important results. To naturalists they have
an especial interest, because Sir John Richardson, who accompanied Franklin as surgeon and naturalist, was one of the most
eminent and successful zoölogical explorers of the century, and
had more to do with the development of our natural history than
any other man not an American.

His natural history papers in Franklin's reports, 1823 and
1828, his " Fauna Boreali Americana," published between 1827
and 1836, his report upon the " Zoölogy of North America," are
all among the classics of our zoölogical literature.*

The third decade was somewhat marked by a renewal of interest in zoölogy and botany, which had, during the few preced-
ing years, been rather overshadowed by geology and mineralogy.

Rafinesque had retired to Kentucky, where, from his professor's chair in Transylvania University, he was issuing his *Annals of Nature* and his *Western Minerva;* and his brilliancy
being dimmed by distance, other students of animals had a
chance to work.

One of the most noteworthy of the workers was Thomas Say
[b. 1787, d. 1834], who was a pioneer in several departments of
systematic zoölogy. A kinsman of the Bartrams, he spent many
of his boyhood days in the old botanic garden at Kingsessing,
in company with the old naturalist, William Bartram, and the
ornithologist Wilson. At the age of twenty-five, having been
unsuccessful as an apothecary, he gave his whole time to
zoölogy. He slept in the hall of the Academy of Natural

* See Rev. John McIlwraith's Life of Sir John Richardson, C. B.,
LL. D. London, 1868. Also Obituary in *London Reader*, 1865, p. 707.

Sciences, where he made his bed beneath the skeleton of a horse, and fed himself upon bread and milk. He was wont, we are told, to regard eating as an inconvenient interruption to scientific pursuits, and to wish that he had been created with a hole in his side, through which his food might be introduced into his system. He built up the museum of the society, and made extensive contributions to biological science.

His article on conchology, published in 1816 in the American edition of Nicholson's Cyclopædia, was the foundation of that science in this country, and was republished in Philadelphia in 1819, with the title, "A Description of the Land and Fresh-water Shells of the United States."

" This work." remarked a contemporary, " ought to be in the possession of every American lover of Natural Science. It has been quoted by *M. Lamarck* and adopted by *M. de Ferrusac*, and has thus taken its place in the scientific world."

Such was fame in America in the year of grace 1820.

In 1817 he did a similar service for systematic entomology, and his contributions to herpetology, to the study of marine invertebrates, especially the crustacea, and to that of invertebrate paleontology, were equally fundamental.

As naturalist of Long's expeditions he described many Western vertebrates, and also collected Indian vocabularies, and it is said that the narrative of the expeditions was chiefly based upon the contents of his note-books.

In 1825 he removed from Philadelphia to New Harmony, Indiana, and, in company with Maclure and Troost, became a member of the community founded there by Owen of Lanark. Comparatively little was thenceforth done by him, and we can only regret the untimely close of so brilliant a career.*

---

* See Memoirs by B. H. Coates, read before American Philosophical Society, Dec. 16, 1834. Memoirs by George Ord; also a tribute to his memory in Dall's presidential address before the Society in January, 1888

Charles Alexander Lesueur [b. at Havre-de-Grace, France, Jan. 1, 1778, d. at Havre, Dec. 12, 1846], the friend and associate of Maclure and Say, accompanied them to New Harmony. The romantic life of this talented Frenchman has been well narrated in his biography by Ord.* He was one of the staff of the Baudin expedition to Australia in 1800, and to his efforts, seconding those of Peron, his associate, were due most of the scientific results which France obtained from that ill-fated enterprise. Lesueur, though a naturalist of considerable ability, was, above all, an artist. The magnificent plates in the reports prepared by Peron † and Freycinet ‡ were all his. He was called " the Raffaelle of zoölogical painters," and his removal to America in 1815 was greatly deplored by European naturalists. He travelled for three years with Maclure, exploring the West Indies and the eastern United States, making a magnificent collection of drawings of fishes and invertebrates, and in 1818 settled in Philadelphia, where, supporting himself by giving drawing lessons, he became an active member of the Academy of Sciences, and published many papers in its Journal.

No one ever drew such exquisite figures of fishes as Lesueur, and it is greatly to be regretted that he never completed his projected work upon North American Ichthyology. He issued a prospectus, with specimen plates, of a " Memoir on the Medusæ," and his name will always be associated with the earliest American work upon marine invertebrates and invertebrate paleontology, because it was to him that Say undoubtedly owed his first acquaintance with these departments of zoölogy. In 1820, while at Albany in the service of the United States and Canadian Boundary Commission, he gave lessons to Eaton and identified his fossils, thus laying the foundations for the future work of the rising school of New ·York paleontologists.

---

* ORD : Memoir of Charles Alexander Lesueur. *Am. Jour. Sci.*, 2d ser., viii, p. 189.
† Voyage des Decouvertes aux Terres Australes.
‡ Voyage aux Terres Australes.

Twelve years of his life were wasted at New Harmony, and in 1837, after the death of Say, he returned to France, carrying his collections and drawings to the Natural History Museum at Havre, of which he became Curator. His period of productiveness was limited to the six years of his residence in Philadelphia. But for their sacrifice to the socialistic ideas of Owen, Say and Lesueur would doubtless be counted among the most distinguished of our naturalists, and the course of American zoölogical research would have been entirely different.

The Rev. Daniel H. Barnes [b. 1785, d. 1828], of New York, a graduate of Union College and a Baptist preacher, was one of Say's earliest disciples, and from 1823 he published papers on conchology, beginning with an elaborate study of the fresh-water mussels. This group was taken up in 1827 by Dr. Isaac Lea, and discussed from year to year in his well-known series of beautifully illustrated monographs.

Mr. Barnes published, also, papers on the " Classification of the Chitonidæ," on " Batrachian Animals and Doubtful Reptiles," and on " Magnetic Polarity."

The officers of the Navy had already begun their contributions to natural history which have been so serviceable in later years. One of the earliest contributions by Barnes was a description of five species of *Chiton* collected in Peru by Capt. C. S. Ridgely, of the " Constellation."

In this period (1828+) was begun the publication of Audubon's folio volumes of illustrations of North American birds— a most extraordinary work, of which Cuvier enthusiastically exclaimed: " C'est le plus magnifique monument que l'Art ait encore élevé a la Nature."

Wilson was the Wordsworth of American naturalists, but Audubon was their Rubens. With pen as well as with brush he delineated those wonderful pictures which have been the delight of the world.

Born in 1781, in Louisiana, while it was still a Spanish colony, he became, at an early age, a pupil of the famous French painter David, under whose tuition he acquired the rudiments of his art. Returning to America, he began the career of an explorer, and for over half a century his life was spent, for the most part, in the forests or in the preparation of his ornithological publications—occasionally visiting England and France, where he had many admirers. His devotion to his work was as complete and self-sacrificing as that of Bowditch, the story of whose translation of LaPlace has already been referred to. It was a great surprise to his friends (though his own fervor did not permit him to doubt) that the sale of his folio volumes was sufficient to pay his printer's bills. Audubon was not a very accomplished systematic zoölogist, and when serious discriminations of species was necessary, sometimes formed alliances with others. Thus Bachman became his collaborator in the study of mammals, and the youthful Baird was invited by him, shortly before his death in 1851, to join him in an ornithological partnership. His relations with Alexander Wilson form the subject of a most entertaining narration in the " Ornithological Biography."*

Thomas Nuttall [b. in Yorkshire, 1786, d. at St. Helens, Lancashire, Sept. 10, 1859] was so thoroughly identified with American natural history and so entirely unconnected with that of England that, although he returned to his native land to die, we may fairly claim him as one of our own worthies. He crossed the ocean when about twenty-one years of age, and travelled in every part of the United States and in the Sandwich Islands studying birds and plants. From 1822 to 1828 he was curator and lecturer at the Harvard Botanical Garden. Besides numerous papers in the Proceedings of the Philadelphia Academy, he published in Philadelphia, in 1818, his " Genera of North

---

* 1, p. 439.

American Plants," in his " Geological Sketch of the Valley of
the Mississippi," in 1821 ; his " Journal of Travels into the Arkansas Territory," a work abounding in natural history observations ; in 1832-4 his " Manual of the Ornithology of the United
States and Canada ;" and in 1843-9 his " North American Sylva,"
a continuation of the Sylva of Michaux. About 1850 he retired
to a rural estate in England, where he died in 1859.

Nuttall was not great as a botanist, as a geologist, or a zoölogist, but was a man useful, beloved, and respected.

Richard Harlan, M. D. [b. 1796, d. 1843], who, with Mitchill,
Say, Rafinesque, and Gosse, was one of the earliest of our herpetolo-
gists, and who was one of Audubon's chief friends and supporters,
published in 1825 the first instalment of his " Fauna Americana,"
which treated exclusively of mammals. This was followed, in
1826, by a rival work on mammals, by Godman. Harlan's book
was a compilation, based largely on translations of portions of
Desmarest's " Mammalogie," printed three years before in Paris.
It was so severely criticised that the second portion, which was
to have been devoted to reptiles, was never published, and its
author turned his attention to medical literature. Godman's
" North American Natural History, or Mastology," contained
much original matter, and, though his contemporaries received it
with faint praise, it is the only separate, compact, illustrated
treatise on the mammals of North America ever published, and is
useful to the present day. John D. Godman [b. in Annapolis,
Md., Dec. 20, 1794, d. in Germantown, Pa., Apl. 17, 1830] died
an untimely death, but gave promise of a brilliant and useful
career as a teacher and investigator. His " Rambles of a Naturalist " is one of the best series of essays of the Selborne type
ever produced by an American, and his " American Natural History" is a work of much importance, even to the present day,
embodying as it does a large number of original observations.

Michaux's Sylva was, as we have seen, continued by Nuttall :

Wilson's American Ornithology was, in like manner, continued by Charles Lucien Bonaparte [b. in Paris, May 24, 1803, d. in Paris, July 30, 1857], Prince of Canino, and nephew of Napoleon the First, a master in systematic zoölogy. Bonaparte came to the United States about the year 1822, and returned to Italy in 1828. His contributions to zoölogical science were of great importance. In 1827, he published in Pisa his "Specchio comparativo delle ornithologie di Roma e di Filadelfia," and from 1825 to 1833 his "American Ornithology," containing descriptions of over one hundred species of birds discovered by himself.

The publication of Torrey's "Flora of the Middle and Northern Sections of the United States" was an event of importance, as was also Dr. W. J. Hooker's essay on the Botany of America,* the first general treatise upon the American flora or fauna, by a master abroad, is pretty sure evidence that the work of home naturalists was beginning to tell.

So, also, in a different way, was the appearance in 1829 of the first edition of Mrs. Lincoln's "Familiar Lectures on Botany," a work which did much toward swelling the army of amateur botanists.

Important work was also in progress in geology. Eaton and Beck were carrying on the Van Rensselaer survey of New York, and in 1818 the former published his "Index to the Geology of the Northern States." Prof. Denison Olmstead, of the University of North Carolina, was completing the official survey of that State—the first ever authorized by the government of a State.

Prof. Lardner Vanuxem, of North Carolina, in 1828, made an important advance, being the first to avail himself successfully of paleontology for the determination of the age of several of our formations, and their approximate synchronism with European beds.†

---

* Brewster's Edinburgh Journal of Science, iii, p. 103.
† Gill.

Horace H. Hayden, of Baltimore [b. 1769, d. 1844], published in 1820 "Geological Essays, or an inquiry into some of the geological phenomena to be found in various parts of America and elsewhere,"* which was well received as a contribution to the history of alluvial formations of the globe, and was apparently the first general work on geology published in this country. Silliman said that it should be a text-book in all the schools. He published, also, a "New Method of preserving Anatomical Preparations,"† "A Singular ore of Cobalt and Manganese,"‡ on "The Bare Hills near Baltimore,"∥ and on "Silk Cocoons,"§ and was a founder and vice-president of the Maryland Academy of Sciences.

XV.

In the fourth decade (1830–40) the leading spirits were Silliman, Hare, Olmstead, Hitchcock, Torrey, DeKay, Henry, and Morse.

Among the men just coming into prominence were J. W. Draper, then professor in Hampden Sidney College, in Virginia, the brothers W. B. and H. D. Rogers, A. A. Gould the conchologist, and James D. Dana.

Henry was just making his first discoveries in physics, having, in 1829, pointed out the possibility of electro-magnetism as a motive power, and in 1831 set up his first telegraphic circuit at Albany. In 1832 the United States Coast Survey, discontinued in 1818, was reorganized under the direction of its first chief, Hassler, now advanced in years.¶

The natural history survey of New York was organized by the

---

* Rev. Sill. Journ., iii, 47. Blackwood's Mag., xvi, 420; xvii, 56.
† American Medical Record, 1822.
‡ *Ibid.* 1832.   ∥ Silliman's Journal, 1822.
§ Journ. Amer. Silk Company, 1839.
¶ Proc. Amer. Assoc. Adv. Sci., ii, 163.

State in 1836, and James Hall and Ebenezer Emmons were placed upon its staff.

G. W. Featherstonhaugh [b. 1780, d. 1866] was conducting (1834-5) a Government expedition, exploring the geology of the elevated country between the Missouri and Red rivers and the Wisconsin territories. He bore the name of " United States Geologist," and projected a geological map of the United States, which now, half a century later, is being completed by the U. S. geologist of to-day. Besides his report upon the survey just referred to, Featherstonhaugh printed a " Geological Reconnoissance, in 1835, from Green- Bay to Coteau des Prairies," and a " Canoe Voyage up the Minnay Sotor," in London, 1847.

In 1838 the United States Exploring Expedition under Wilkes was sent upon its voyage of circumnavigation, having upon its staff a young naturalist named Dana, whose studies upon the crustaceans and radiates of the expedition have made him a world-wide reputation, entirely independent of that which he has since gained as a mineralogist and geologist. It is customary to refer to the Wilkes expedition as having been sent out entirely in the interests of science. As a matter of fact it was organized primarily in the interests of the whale fishery of the United States.

Dana, before his departure with Wilkes, had published, in 1837, the first edition of his " System of Mineralogy." a work which, in its subsequent editions, has become the standard manual of the world.

The publication of Lyell's " Principles of Geology " at the beginning of this decade (1830) had given new direction to the thoughts of our geologists, and they were all hard at work under its inspiration.

With 1839 ended the second of our thirty-year periods—the one which I have chosen to speak of as the period of Silliman—not so much because of the investigations of the New Haven professor, as on account of his influence in the promotion of American Science and scientific institutions.

This was a time of hard work, and we must not withhold our praise from the noble little company of pioneers who were, in those years, building the foundations upon which the scientific institutions of to-day are resting.

The difficulties and drawbacks of scientific research at this time have been well described by one who knew them :*

" The professedly scientific institutions of our country issued, from time to time, though at considerable intervals, volumes of transactions and proceedings unquestionably not without their influence in keeping alive the scarcely kindled flame, but whose contents, as might be expected, were, for the most part, rather in conformity with the then existing standard of excellence than in advance of it. Natural history in the United States was the mere sorting of genera and species. The highest requisite for distinction in any physical science was the knowledge of what European students had attained. Astronomy was, in general, confined to observations, and those not of the most refined character, and its merely descriptive departments were estimated far more highly than the study of its laws. Astronomical computation had hardly risen above the ciphering out of eclipses and occultations. Indeed, I risk nothing in saying that astronomy had lost ground in America since those colonial times, when men like Rittenhouse kept up a constant scientific communication with students of astronomy beyond the seas. And I believe I may farther say, that a single instance of a man's devoting himself to science as the only earthly guide, aim, and object of his life, while unassured of a professor's chair or some analogous appointment upon which he might depend for subsistence, was utterly unknown.

" Such was the state of science in general. In astronomy the expensive appliances requisite for all observations of the higher class were wanting, and there was not in the United States, with the exception of the Hudson Observatory, to which Professor Loomis devoted such hours as he could spare from his duties in the college, a single establishment provided with the means of making an absolute determination of the place of any celestial body, or even relative determinations at all commensurate in accuracy with the demands of the times. The only instrument that could be thought of for the purpose was the Yale College telescope, which, although provided with a micrometer, was destitute of the means of identifying comparison-stars. A better idea of American astronomy a dozen years ago can hardly be obtained than by quot-

---

* GOULD, B. A. Address in commemoration of Sears Cook Walker.
<Proc. Amer. Assoc. Ad. Sci., viii, 25

ing from an article published at that time by the eminent geometer who now retires from the position of President of this Association. He will forgive me the liberty for the sake of the illustration. ' The impossibility,' said he, ' of great national progress in astronomy, while the materials are, for the most part, imported, can hardly need to be impressed upon the patrons of science in this country. * * * And next to the support of observers is the establishment of observatories. Something has been done for this purpose in various parts of the country, and it is earnestly to be hoped that the intimations which we have heard regarding the intentions of Government may prove to be well founded ; that we shall soon have a permanent national observatory equal in its appointments to the best furnished ones of Europe ; and that American ships will ere long calculate their longitudes and latitudes from an American nautical almanac. That there is on this side of the Atlantic a sufficient capacity for celestial observations is amply attested by the success which has attended the efforts, necessarily humble which have hitherto been made.'"*

XVI.

Just before the middle of the century a wave, or to speak more accurately, a series of waves of intellectual activity began to pass over Europe and America. There was a renaissance, quite as important as that which occurred in Europe at the close of the Middle Ages. Draper and other historians have pointed out the causes of this movement, prominent among which were the introduction of steam and electricity, annihilating space and relieving mankind from a great burden of mechanical drudgery. It was the beginning of the " age of science," and political as well as social and industrial changes followed in rapid succession.

In Europe the great work began a little earlier. Professor Huxley, in his address to the Royal Society in 1885, took for a fixed point his own birthday in 1825, which was four months before the completion of the railway between Stockton and Darlington—" the ancestral representative of the vast reticulated fetching and carrying organism which now extends its meshes over the civilized world." Since then, he remarked, " the greater

---

* PEIRCE, BENJAMIN, Cambridge Miscellany, 1842, p. 25.

part of the vast body of knowledge which constitutes the modern sciences of physics, chemistry, biology, and geology has been acquired, and the widest generalizations therefrom have been deduced, and, furthermore, the majority of those applications of scientific knowledge to practical ends which have brought about the most striking differences between our present civilization and that of antiquity have been made within that period of time."

It is within the past half century, he continued, that the most brilliant additions have been made to fact and theory and serviceable hypothesis in the region of pure science, for within this time falls the establishment on a safe basis of the greatest of all the generalizations of science, the doctrines of the Conservation of Energy and of Evolution. Within this time the larger moiety of our knowledge of light, heat, electricity, and magnetism has been acquired. Our present chemistry has been, in great part, created, while the whole science has been remodelled from foundation to roof.

" It may be natural," continued Professor Huxley, " that progress should appear most striking to me among those sciences to which my own attention has been directed, but I do not think this will wholly account for the apparent advance ' by leaps and bounds' of the biological sciences within my recollection. The cell theory was the latest novelty when I began to work with the microscope, and I have watched the building of the whole vast fabric of histology. I can say almost as much of embryology, since Von Baer's great work was published in 1828. Our knowledge of the morphology of the lower plants and animals and a great deal of that of the higher forms has very largely been obtained in my time ; while physiology has been put upon a totally new foundation, and, as it were, reconstructed, by the thorough application of the experimental method to the study of the phenomena of life, and by the accurate determination of the purely physical and chemical components of these phenomena.

The exact nature of the processes of sexual and non-sexual repro-
duction has been brought to light. Our knowledge of geographical and geological distribution and of the extinct forms of life
has been increased a hundredfold. As for the progress of geological science, what more need be said than that the first volume
of Lyell's ' Principles ' bears the date of 1830."

It cannot be expected that, within the limits of this address, I
should attempt to show what America has done in the last half
century. I am striving to trace the beginnings, not the results, of
scientific work on this side of the Atlantic. I will simply quote
what was said by the London *Times* in 1876:

"In the natural distribution of subjects, the history of enterprise, discovery, and conquest, and the growth of republics, fell
to America, and she has dealt nobly with them. In the wider
and more multifarious provinces of art and science she runs neck
and neck with the mother country and is never left behind."

It is difficult to determine exactly the year when the first
waves of this renaissance reached the shores of America. Silliman, in his Priestley address, placed the date at 1845. I should
rather say 1840, when the first national scientific association was
organized, although signs of awakening may be detected even before the beginning of the previous decade. We must, however,
carefully avoid giving too much prominence to the influence of
individuals. I have spoken of this period of thirty years as the
period of Agassiz. Agassiz, however, did not bring the waves
with him; he came in on the crest of one of them; he was not
the founder of modern American natural history, but, as a public
teacher and organizer of institutions, he exerted a most important
influence upon its growth.

One of the leading events of the decade was the reorganization
of the Coast Survey in 1844, under the sage administration of
Alexander Dallas Bache,* speedily followed by the beginning of

---

* Proc. Amer. Assoc. Adv. Sci., ii, 164.

investigations upon the Gulf Stream, and of the researches of
Count Pourtales into its fauna, which laid the foundations of mod-
ern deep-sea exploration.   Others were the founding of the
Lawrence Scientific School, the Cincinnati Observatory, the
Yale Analytical Laboratory, the celebration of the Centennial
Jubilee of the American Philosophical Society in 1843, and the
enlargement of Silliman's " American Journal of Science."

The Naval Astronomical Expedition was sent to Chili, under
Gibbon (1849), to make observations upon the parallax of the
sun.   Lieut. Lynch was sent to Palestine (in 1848) at the head
of an expedition to explore the Jordan and the Dead Sea.

Frémont conducted expeditions, in 1848, to explore the
Rocky Mountains and the territory beyond, and Stansbury, in
1849-'50, a similar exploration of the valley of the Great Salt
Lake.   David Dale Owen was heading a Government Geological
Survey in Wisconsin, Iowa, and Minnesota (1848), and from all
of these came results of importance to science and to natural
history.

In 1849, Prof. W. H. Harvey, of Dublin, visited America and
collected materials for his *Nereis Boreali-Americana*, which
was the foundation of our marine botany.

Sir Charles Lyell, ex-President of the Geological Society
of London, visited the United States in 1841 and again in 1845,
and published two volumes of travels, which were, however, of
much less importance than the effects of his encouraging presence
upon the rising school of American geologists.   His " Principles
of Geology," as has already been said, was an epoch-making
work, and he was to his generation almost what Darwin was to
the one which followed.

Certain successes of our astronomers and physicists had a bearing upon the progress of American science in all its departments,
which was, perhaps, even greater than their actual importance
would seem to warrant.   These were the discovery, by the Bards

of Cambridge, of Bards comet in 1846, of the satellite Hyperion in 1848, of the third ring of Saturn in 1850, the discovery by Herrick and Bradley, in 1846, of the bi-partition of Belas comet, and the application of the telegraph to longitude determination after Locke had constructed, in 1848, his clock for the registration of time observations by means of electro-magnetism.

It is almost ludicrous at this day to observe the grateful sentiments with which our men of science welcomed the adoption of this American method in the observatory at Greenwich.

Americans were still writhing under the sting of Sidney Smith's demand " Who reads an American book?" and the narrations of those critical observers of national customs, Dickens, Basil Hall, and Mrs. Trollope.

The continental approval of American science was like balsam to the sensitive spirits of our countrymen.

John William Draper's versatile and original researches in physics were also yielding weighty results, and as early as 1847 he had already laid the foundations of the science of spectroscopy which Kirchhoff so boldly appropriated many years later.

Most important of all, by reason of its breadth of scope, was the foundation of the Smithsonian Institution, which was organized in 1846 by the election of Joseph Henry to its secretaryship. Who can attempt to say what the conditions of science in the United States would be to-day, but for the bequest of Smithson? In the words of John Quincy Adams, "Of all the foundations or establishments for pious or charitable uses which ever signalized the spirit of the age or the comprehensive beneficence of the founder, none can be named more deserving the approbation of mankind."

Among the leaders of this new enterprise and of the scientific activities of the day may be named: Silliman, Hare, Henry, Bache, Maury, Alexander, Locke, Mitchel, Peirce, Walker, Draper, Dana, Wyman, Agassiz, Gray, Torrey, Haldeman,

Morton, Holbrook, Gibbes, Gould, DeKay, Storer, Hitchcock, Redfield, the brothers Rogers, Jackson, Hays, and Owen.

Among the rising men were Baird, Adams the conchologist, Burnett, Harris the entomologist, and the LeConte brothers among zoölogists; Lapham, D. C. Eaton, and Grant, among botanists; Sterry Hunt, Brush, J. D. Whitney, Wolcott Gibbs, and Lesley, among chemists and geologists, as well as Schiel, of St. Louis, who had before 1842 discovered the principle of chemical homology.

I have not time to say what ought to be said of the coming of Agassiz in 1846. He lives in the hearts of his adopted countrymen. He has a colossal monument in the museum which he reared, and a still greater one in the lives and works of pupils such as Agassiz, Allen, Burgess, Burnett, Brooks, Clarke. Cooke, Faxon, Fewkes, Gorman, Hartt, Hyatt, Joseph LeConte, Lyman, McCrady, Morse, Mills, Niles, Packard, Putnam, Scudder, St. John, Shaler, Verrill, Wilder, and David A. Wells.

XVII.

They were glorious men who represented American science at the middle of the century. We may well wonder whether the present decade will make as good a showing forty years hence.

The next decade was its continuation. The old leaders were nearly all active, and to their ranks were added many more.

An army of new men was rising up.

It was a period of great explorations, for the frontier of the United States was sweeping westward, and there was need of a better knowledge of the public domain.

Sitgreaves explored the region of the Zuñi and Colorado rivers in 1852, and Marcy the Red River of the North. The Mexican boundary survey, under Emory, was in progress from 1854 to 1856, and at the same time the various Pacific railroad surveys. There was also the Herndon exploration of the valley of the Amazon, and the North Pacific exploring expedition under Rogers. These were the days, too, when that extensive exploration of British North America was begun, through the co-operation of the Hudson's Bay Company with the Smithsonian Institution.

It was the harvest-time of the museums. Agassiz was building up with immense rapidity his collections in Cambridge, utilizing to the fullest extent the methods which he had learned in the great European establishments and the public spirit and generosity of the Americans. Baird was using his matchless powers of organization in equipping and inspiring the officers of the various surveys, and accumulating immense collections to be used in the interest of the future National Museum.

Systematic natural history advanced with rapid strides. The magnificent folio reports of the Wilkes expedition were now being published, and some of them, particularly those by Dana on the crustaceans and the zoöphytes and geology, that of Gould upon the mollusks, those by Torrey, Gray, and Eaton upon the plants, were of great importance.

The reports of the domestic surveys contained numerous papers upon systematic natural history, prepared under the direction of Baird, assisted by Girard, Gill, Cassin, Suckley, LeConte, Cooper, and others. The volumes relating to the mammals and the birds, prepared by Baird's own pen, were the first exhaustive treatises upon the mammalogy and ornithology of the United States.

The American Association was doing a great work in popular education through its system of meeting each year in a different city. In 1850 it met in Charleston, and its entire expenses were paid by the city corporation as a valid mark of public approval, while the foundation of the Charleston museum of natural history was one of the direct results of the meeting.

In 1857 it met in Montreal, and delegates from the English scientific societies were present; this was one of the earliest of those manifestations of international courtesy upon scientific ground of which there have since been many.

In the seventh decade, which began with threatenings of civil war, the growth of science was almost arrested. A meeting of the American Association was to have been held in Nashville in 1861, but none was called. In 1866, at Buffalo, its sessions were resumed with the old board of officers elected in 1860. One of the vice-presidents, Gibbes, of South Carolina, had not been heard from since the war began, and the Southern members were all absent. Many of the Northern members wrote, explaining that they could not attend this meeting because they could not afford it, "such had been the increase of living expenses, without a corresponding increase in the salaries of men of science." Few scientists were engaged in the war, though one, O. M. Mitchel, who left the directorship of the Dudley observatory to accept the command of an Ohio brigade, died in service in 1862, and another, Couthouy, sacrificed his life in the navy. Others, like Ordway, left the ranks of science never to resume their places as investigators.

Scientific effort was paralyzed, and attention was directed to other matters. In 1864, when the Smithsonian building was burned, Lincoln, it is said, looking at the flames from the windows of the Executive Mansion, remarked to some military officers who were present: "Gentlemen, yonder is a national calamity. We have no time to think about it now. We must attend to other things."

The only important events during the war were two; one the organization of the National Academy of Sciences, which soon became what Bache had remarked the necessity for in 1851, when he said: "An institution of science, supplementary to existing ones, is much needed to guide public action in reference to scientific matters."[*]

The other was the passage, in 1862, of the bill for the establishment of scientific educational institutions in every State.

---

* Proc. Amer. Assoc. Adv. Sci., vi, xlviii.

The agricultural colleges were then, as they still are, unpopular among many scientific men, but the wisdom of the measure is apparently before long to be justified.

Before the end of the decade, the Northern States* had begun a career of renewed prosperity, and the scientific institutions were reorganized. The leading spirits were such men as Pierce, Henry, Agassiz, Gray, Barnard, the Goulds, Newberry, Lea, Whittlesey, Foster, Rood, Cooke, Newcomb, Newton, Wyman, Winchell.

Among the rising men, some of them very prominent before 1870, were Barker, Bolton, Chandler, Eggleston, Hall, Harkness, Langley, Mayer, Pickering, Young, Powell, Pumpelly, Abbe, Collett, Emerson, Hartt, Lupton, Marsh, Whitfield, Williams, N. H. Winchell, Agassiz, the Allens, Beale, Cope, Coues, Canby, Dall, Hoy, Hyatt, Morse, Orton, Perkins, Rey, Riley, Scudder, Sidney Smith, Stearns, Tuttle, Verrill, Wood.

Soon after the war the surveys of the West, which have coalesced to form the U. S. Geological Survey, were forming under the direction of Clarence Cook, Lieut. Wheeler, F. V. Hayden, and Major Powell.

The discovery of the nature of the corona of the sun by Young and Harkness in 1869 was an event encouraging to the rising spirits of our workers.

XVIII.

With 1869 we reach the end of the third period and the threshold of that in which we are living. I shall not attempt to define the characteristics of the natural history of to-day, though I wish to direct attention to certain tendencies and conditions which exist. Let me, however, refer once more to the past, since it leads again directly up to the present.

---

* See A D WHITE's Scientific and Industrial Education in the United States. < Popular Science Monthly, v, p. 170.

In a retrospect published in 1876,* one of our leaders stated
that American science during the first forty years of the present
century was in " a state of general lethargy, broken now and
then by the activity of some first-class man, which, however,
commonly ceased to be directed into purely scientific channels."
This depiction was, no doubt, somewhat true of the physical
and mathematical sciences concerned, but not to the extent indicated by the writer quoted. What could be more unjust to the
men of the last generation than this? " It is," continues he,
" strikingly illustrative of the absence of everything like an
effective national pride in science that two generations should
have passed without America having produced anything to con-
tinue the philosophical researches of Franklin."

I may not presume to criticise the opinion of the writer from
whom these words are quoted, but I cannot resist the tempta-
tion to repeat a paragraph from Prof. John W. Draper's eloquent
centennial address upon " Science in America :"

" In many of the addresses on the centennial occasion," he
said, " the shortcomings of the United States in extending the
boundaries of scientific knowledge, especially in the physical and
chemical departments, have been set forth. ' We must acknowl-
edge with shame our inferiority to other people,' says one. ' We
have done nothing,' says another. * * * But we must not
forget that many of these humiliating accusations are made by
persons who are not of authority in the matter ; who, because
they are *ignorant* of what has been done, *think* that nothing
has been done. They mistake what is merely a blank in their
own information for a blank in reality. In their alacrity to de-
preciate the merit of their own country they would have us confess
that, for the last century, we have been living on the reputation
of Franklin and his thunder-rod."

These are the words of one who, himself an Englishman by
birth, could, with excellent grace, upbraid our countrymen for
their lack of patriotism.

The early American naturalists have been reproached for de-

* North American Review.

voting their time to explorations and descriptive natural history, and their work depreciated, as being of a character beneath the dignity of the biologists of to-day.

" The zoölogical science of the country," said the president of the Natural History Section of the American Association a few years since, " presents itself in two distinct periods : The first period may be recognized as embracing the lowest stages of the science ; it included, among others, a class of men who busied themselves in taking an inventory of the animals of the country, an important and necessary work to be compared to that of the hewers and diggers who first settle a new country, but in their work demanded no deep knowledge or breadth of view."

It is quite unnecessary to defend systematic zoölogy from such slurs as this, nor do I believe that the writer quoted would really defend the ideas which his words seem to convey, although, as Professor Judd has regretfully confessed in his recent address before the Geological Society of London, systematic zoölogists and botanists have become somewhat rare and out of fashion in Europe in modern times.

The best vindication of the wisdom of our early writers will be, I think, the presentation of a counter-quotation from another presidential address, that of the venerable Dr. Bentham before the Linnæan Society of London, in 1867 :

" It is scarcely half a century," wrote Bentham, " since our American brethren applied themselves in earnest to the investigation of the natural productions and physical condition of their vast continent ; their progress, especially during the latter half of that period, had been very rapid until the outbreak of the recent war, so deplorable in its effects in the interests of science as well as on the material prosperity of their country. The peculiar condition of the North American Continent requires imperatively that its physical and biological statistics should be accurately collected and authentically recorded, and that this should be speedily done. It is more than any country, except our Australian colonies, in a state of transition. Vast tracts of land are still in what may be called almost a primitive state, unmodified by the effects of civilization, uninhabited, or tenanted only by the remnants of ancient tribes, whose unsettled life never exercised much influence over the natural productions of the country. But this state of things is rapidly passing away; the invasion and steady progress of a civilized population, whilst changing generally the face of nature, is obliterating many of the evidences of a former state of things. It may be true that the call for recording the traces of previous conditions may be particularly strong in Ethnology and Archæology; but in our own branches of the science, the observations and consequent theories of Darwin having called special attention to the history of species, it becomes particularly important that accurate biological statistics should be obtained for future comparison in those countries where the circumstances influencing those conditions are the most rapidly changing. The larger races of wild animals are dwindling down, like the aboriginal inhabitants, under the deadly influence of civilized man. Myriads of the lower orders of animal life, as well as of plants, disappear with the destruction of forests, the drainage of swamps, and the gradual spread of cultivation, and their places are occupied by foreign invaders. Other races, no doubt, without actually disappearing, undergo a gradual change under the new order of things, which, if perceptible only in the course of successive generations, require so much the more for future proof an accurate record of their state in the still unsettled condition of the country. In the Old World almost every attempt to compare the present state of vegetation or animal life with that which existed in uncivilized times is in a great measure frustrated by the absolute want of evidence as to that former state; but in North America the change is going forward, as it were, close under the eye of the observer. This consideration may one day give great value to the reports of the naturalist sent by the Government, as we have seen, at the instigation of the Smithsonian Institution and other promoters of science, to accompany the surveys of new territories."

Having said this much in defence of the scientific men of the United States, I wish, in conclusion, to prefer some very serious charges against the country at large, or, rather, as a citizen of the United States, to make some very melancholy and humiliating confessions.

The present century is often spoken of as " the age of science," and Americans are somewhat disposed to be proud of the mannei in which scientific institutions are fostered and scientific investigators encouraged on this side of the Atlantic.

Our countrymen have made very important advances in many

departments of research.   We have a few admirably organized
laboratories and observatories, a few good collections of scientific
books, six or eight museums worthy of the name, and a score or
more of scientific and technological schools, well organized and
better provided with officers than with money.   We have several
strong scientific societies, no one of which, however, publishes
transactions worthy of its own standing and the collective reputation of its members.   In fact, the combined publishing funds of all
our societies would not pay for the annual issue of a volume of
memoirs, such as appears under the auspices of any one of a dozen
European societies which might be named.

Our Government, by a liberal support of its scientific departments, has done much to atone for the really feeble manner in
which local institutions have been maintained.   The Coast Survey, the Geological Surveys, the Department of Agriculture, the
Fish Commissions, the Army, with its Meteorological Bureau, its
Medical Museum and Library, and its explorations; the Navy,
with its Observatory, its laboratories and its explorations; and in
addition to these, the Smithsonian Institution, with its systematic
promotion of all good works in science, have accomplished more
than is ordinarily placed to their credit.   Many hundreds of volumes of scientific memoirs have been issued from the Government
printing office since 1870, and these have been distributed in such
a generous and far-reaching way that they have not failed to reach
every town and village in the United States where a roof has been
provided to protect them.

It may be that some one will accuse the Government of having
usurped the work of the private publisher.   Very little of value
in the way of scientific literature has been issued during the same
period by publishers, except in reprints or translations of works
of foreign investigators.   It should be borne in mind, however,
that our Government has not only published the results of investigations, but has supported the investigators and provided them

with laboratories, instruments and material, and that the memoirs which it has issued would never, as a rule, have been accepted by private publishers.

I do not wish to underrate the efficiency of American men of science, nor the enthusiasm with which many public men and capitalists have promoted our scientific institutions. Our countrymen have had wonderful successes in many directions. They have borne their share in the battle of science against the unknown. They have had abundant recognition from their fellow-workers in the Old World. They have met perhaps a more intelligent appreciation abroad than at home. It is the absence of home appreciation that causes us very much foreboding for the future.

In Boston or Cambridge, in New York, Philadelphia, Baltimore, Washington, Chicago, or San Francisco, and in most of the college towns, a man interested in science may find others ready to talk over with him a new scientific book, or a discovery which has excited his interest. Elsewhere, the chances are, he will have to keep his thoughts to himself. One may quickly recite the names of the towns and cities in which may be found ten or more people whose knowledge of any science is aught than vague and rudimentary. Let me illustrate my idea by supposing that every inhabitant of the United States, over fifteen years of age, should be required to mention ten living men eminent in scientific work, would one out of a hundred be able to respond? Does any one suppose that there are three or four hundred thousand people enlightened to this degree?

Let us look at some statistics, or, rather, some facts, which it is convenient to arrange in statistical form. The total number of white inhabitants of the United States in 1880 was about forty-two millions. The total number of naturalists, as shown in the *Naturalist's Directory* for 1886, was a little over 4,600. This list includes not only the investigators, who probably do not exceed five hundred in number, and the advanced teachers, who muster, perhaps, one thousand strong, but all who are sufficiently interested in science to have selected special lines of study.

We have, then, one person interested in science to about ten thousand inhabitants. But the leaven of science is not evenly distributed through the national loaf. It is the tendency of scientific men to congregate together. In Washington, for instance, there is one scientific man to every 500 inhabitants, in Cambridge one to 850, and in New Haven one to 1,100. In New Orleans the proportion is one to 8,800, in Jersey City one to 24,000, in New York one to 7,000, and in Brooklyn one to 8,500. I have before me the proportions worked out for the seventy-five principal cities of the United States. The showing is suggestive, though no doubt in some instances misleading. The tendency to gregariousness on the part of scientific men may, perhaps, be further illustrated by a reference to certain societies. The membership of the National Academy of Sciences is almost entirely concentrated about Boston, New York, Philadelphia, Washington and New Haven. Missouri has one member, Illinois one, Ohio one, Maryland, New Jersey and Rhode Island three, and California four—while thirty-two States and Territories are not represented. A precisely similar distribution of members is found in the American Society of Naturalists. A majority of the members of the American Association for the Advancement of Science live in New York, Massachusetts, Pennsylvania, the District of Columbia, Michigan, Minnesota, Ohio, Illinois and New Jersey.

It has been stated that the average proportion of scientific men to the population at large is one to ten thousand. A more minute examination shows that while fifteen of the States and Territories have more than the average proportion of scientific men, thirty-two have less. Oregon and California, Michigan and Delaware have very nearly the normal number. Massachusetts, Rhode Island, Connecticut, Illinois, Colorado and Florida have about one to four thousand. West Virginia, Nevada, Arkansas,

Mississippi, Georgia, Kentucky, Texas, Alabama and the Carolinas are the ones least liberally furnished. Certain cities appear to be absolutely without scientific men. The worst cases of destitution seem to be Paterson, New Jersey, a city of 50,000 inhabitants, Wheeling, with 30,000, Quincy, Illinois, with 26,000, Newport, Kentucky, with 20,000, Williamsport, Pennsylvania, and Kingston, New York, with 18,000, Council Bluffs, Iowa, and Zanesville, Ohio, with 17,000, Oshkosh and Sandusky, with 15,000, Lincoln, Rhode Island, Norwalk, Connecticut, and Brockton and Pittsfield, Massachusetts, with 13,000. In these there are no men of science recorded, and eight cities of more than 15,000 inhabitants have only one, namely, Omaha, Nebraska, and St. Joseph, Missouri, Chelsea, Massachusetts, Cohoes, New York, Sacramento, California, Binghamton, New York, Portland, Oregon, and Leadville, Colorado.

Of course these statistical statements are not properly statistics. I have no doubt that some of these cities are misrepresented in what has been said. This much, however, is probably true, that not one of them has a scientific society, a museum, a school of science, or a sufficient number of scientific men to insure even the occasional delivery of a course of scientific lectures.

Studying the distribution of scientific societies, we find that there are fourteen States and Territories in which there are no scientific societies whatever. There are fourteen States which have State academies of science or societies which are so organized as to be equivalent to State academies.

Perhaps the most discouraging feature of all is the diminutive circulation of scientific periodicals. In addition to a certain number of specialists' journals, we have in the United States three which are wide enough in scope to be necessary to all who attempt to keep an abstract of the progress of science. Of these, the *American Journal of Science* has, we are told, a circulation of less than 800; the *American Naturalist*, less than 1,100, and *Science*, less than 6,000. A considerable proportion of the copies printed go, as a matter of course, to public institutions, and not to individuals. Even the *Popular Science Monthly* and the *Scientific American*, which appeal to large classes of unscientific readers, have circulations absurdly small. The most effective agents for the dissemination of scientific intelligence are, probably, the religious journals, aided to some extent by the agricultural journals, and to a very limited degree by the weekly and daily newspapers. It is much to be regretted that several influential journals, which ten or fifteen years ago gave attention to the publication of trustworthy scientific intelligence, have of late almost entirely abandoned the effort. The allusions to science in the majority of our newspapers are singularly inaccurate and unscholarly, and too often science is referred to only when some of its achievements offer opportunity for witticism.

The statements which I have just made may, as I have said, prove, in some instances erroneous, and, to some extent, misleading, but I think the general tendency of a careful study of the distribution of scientific men and institutions is to show that the people of the United States, except in so far as they sanction by their approval the work of the scientific departments of the Government, and the institutions established by private munificence, have little reason to be proud of the national attitude toward science.

I am, however, by no means despondent for the future. The importance of scientific work is thoroughly appreciated, and it is well understood that many important public duties can be performed properly only by trained men of science. The claims of science to a prominent place in every educational plan are every year more fully conceded. Science is permeating the theory and the practice of every art and every industry, as well as every department of learning. The greatest danger to science is, perhaps, the fact that all who have studied at all within the last quarter of a century have studied its rudiments and feel competent to employ its methods and its language, and to form judgments on the merits of current work.

In the meantime the professional men of science, the scholars, and the investigators seem to me to be strangely indifferent to the questions as to how the public at large is to be made familiar with the results of their labors. It may be that the tendency to specialization is destined to deprive the sciences of their former hold upon popular interest, and that the study of zoölogy, botany and geology, mineralogy and chemistry will become so technical that each will require the exclusive attention of its votaries for a period of years. It may be that we are to have no more zoölogists such as Agassiz and Baird, no more botanists such as Gray, and that the place which such men filled in the community will be supplied by combinations of a number of specialists, each of whom knows, with more minuteness, limited portions of the subjects grasped bodily by the masters of the last generation. It may be that the use of the word naturalist is to became an anachronism, and that we are all destined to become, generically biologists, and, specifically, morphologists, histologists, embryologists, physiologists, or, it may be, cetologists, chiropterologists, oölogists, carcinologists, ophiologists, helminthologists, actinologists, coleopterists, caricoölogists, mycologists, muscologists, bacteriologists, diatomologists, paleo-botanists, crystallographers, petrologists, and the like.

I can but believe, however, that it is the duty of every scientific scholar, however minute his specialty, to resist in himself, and in the professional circles which surround him, the tendency toward narrowing technicality in thought and sympathy, and above all in the education of non-professional students.

I cannot resist the feeling that American men of science are in a large degree responsible if their fellow-citizens are not fully awake to the claims of scientific endeavor in their midst.

I am not in sympathy with those who feel that their dignity is lowered when their investigations lead toward improvement in the physical condition of mankind, but I feel that the highest function of science is to minister to their mental and moral welfare. Here in the United States, more than in any other country, it is necessary that sound, accurate knowledge and a scientific manner of thought should exist among the people, and the man of science is becoming, more than ever, the natural custodian of the treasured knowledge of the world. To him, above all others, falls the duty of organizing and maintaining the institutions for the diffusion of knowledge, many of which have been spoken of in these addresses—the schools, the museums, the expositions, the societies, the periodicals. To him, more than to any other American, should be made familiar the words of President Washington in his farewell address to the American people :

"PROMOTE, THEN, AS AN OBJECT OF PRIMARY IMPORTANCE, INSTITUTIONS FOR THE GENERAL DIFFUSION OF KNOWLEDGE. IN PROPORTION AS THE STRUCTURE OF A GOVERNMENT GIVES FORCE TO PUBLIC OPINIONS IT SHOULD BE ENLIGHTENED.

www.ingramcontent.com/pod-product-compliance
Lightning Source LLC
Chambersburg PA
CBHW021421090426
42742CB00009B/1205